OPTION SELLING *for* Profit

The Builder's Guide to Generating Design Center Revenue and Profit

Gina Gullo and
Angela Rinaldi

BuilderBooks.com®
BOOKS THAT BUILD YOUR BUSINESS
A Service of NAHB®
National Association of Home Builders

Option Selling for Profit

The Builder's Guide to Generating Design Center Revenue and Profit

BuilderBooks, a Service of the National Association of Home Builders

Courtenay S. Brown	Director, Book Publishing
Natalie C. Holmes	Book Editor
Torrie Singletary	Production Editor
Circle Graphics	Cover Design
Circle Graphics	Composition
McNaughton & Gunn	Printing
Gerald M. Howard	NAHB Executive Vice President and CEO
Mark Pursell	NAHB Senior Staff Vice President, Marketing & Sales Group
Lakisha Campbell	NAHB Staff Vice President, Publications & Affinity Programs

Printed in the United States of America

12 11 10 09   1 2 3 4 5

Library of Congress Cataloging-in-Publication Data

Gullo, Gina, 1958-
 Option selling for profit: The builder's guide to generating design center
revenue and profit / Gina Gullo and Angela Rinaldi.
  p. cm.
 Includes bibliographical references and index.
 ISBN 978-0-86718-642-0
 1. Construction industry—Customer services. 2. House construction. 3.
Architectural design. 4. Interior decoration. I. Rinaldi, Angela, 1952- II. Title.

HD9715.A2G926 2008
690.068'1—dc22

2008012844

For further information, please contact:

BuilderBooks.com®
BOOKS THAT BUILD YOUR BUSINESS
A Service of NAHB® National Association of Home Builders

National Association of Home Builders
1201 15th Street, NW
Washington, DC 20005-2800
800-223-2665
www.BuilderBooks.com.

Contents

Preface

Option selling is arguably the most important customer service and profit opportunity in home building today. During slow housing markets proactive builders use their design centers to entice prospective home buyers. The community salesperson, in anticipation of selling the customer a home, sends them to the design center to preview the exciting option program. Therefore, the design center is a critical component of the customer experience and an essential tool for raising profit.

Without a finely tuned plan for rolling out a successful option program once the customer gets to the design center, a builder risks internal miscommunication, costly errors, crippling delays, and most importantly, customer dissatisfaction and lost profit. Too often in the home building industry convoluted processes and poor internal communication lead to a customer experience that is downright maddening. If you don't believe it, follow along with us as we recount a true story—one that is not unique within the home building industry.

A national builder introduced a condominium product for a premier community. The new location was ideal, the market was strong, and the project sold out unexpectedly rapidly—in a matter of weeks. With all units sold, the project management team saw an opportunity to cut carrying costs and hastily moved ahead to condense the production schedule. Instead of taking two years, the project would now be completed, and all sales closed, within 14 months. This was an opportunity to end the year with remarkable results; what a feat it would be! While this rapid-response approach looked reasonable on paper, it turned out to be a nightmare.

Realizing their time crunch, the project managers concluded that all 90 option selection appointments would have to be scheduled and contracts would have to be finalized within 90 days. Therefore, the builder hurriedly (and prematurely) approved an incomplete option program, while ordering the design center and customers to accommodate the new schedule. Specifically, the design center was instructed to alert customers that they would close with a standard builder interior if their selections were not completed within three months. This ultimatum did not sit well with customers who had just spent, on average, $450,000 for a condo and had originally been told that their move-in dates were at least a year and a half away. Nevertheless, customers grudgingly rearranged their schedules to meet the nearly impossible timetable. Because many of them were not local, they had to arrange last-minute flights and hotel stays in order to meet the strict deadlines.

While the customers were in a frenzy trying to meet the new deadline, the builder's purchasing department was still in the process of selecting products and pricing for the previously approved option program. This piecemeal pricing resulted in repeated revisions to option contracts. After option pricing was supposedly completed, the next six months were fraught with countless errors, oversights, and mistakes, including

- multiple pricing errors
- discrepancies between products the builder listed in the option program and what trade partners had agreed to supply

- options that could not be installed due to architectural plan errors
- orders placed for products before option contracts were finalized and signed
- incorrect model numbers assigned to options

Mayhem in the design center ensued as frustrated, angry customers were asked to make their option selections without complete pricing. Customers became suspicious about the builder's integrity.

Behind the scenes, various departments were bickering, pointing fingers, and causing permanent customer service damage. The trade partners were angry because they absorbed added costs. The builder was angry because the company was forced to issue refunds and rip out and replace incorrect options. Valuable time was spent retracing steps to correct errors and rebuild customer relations. The final blow was that all of the chaos was just wasted effort; the aggressive project schedule was not met.

Although the customers had held up their end of the bargain, the requirements they fulfilled and deadlines they met did not get them their new homes any sooner. They felt tricked after realizing they were forced to move through the option selection process at warp speed without purpose or reason.

This true story and many others like it were the reason and inspiration for this book. Builders who repeat these mistakes risk internal company anguish, a miserable customer experience, and lost profits. Ineffective option sales programs—those that are poorly planned and out of sync with market demand—will eat away at your profit margin. Instead, builders must adopt a retail philosophy for selling options—one that embraces consumers as their most valuable asset and advertisement, and then caters to their tastes, experiences, and buying habits accordingly.

Acknowledgments

The authors would like to acknowledge the following individuals for their contributions to *Option Selling for Profit: The Builder's Guide to Generating Design Center Revenue and Profit*: Mary DeWalt, president, Mary DeWalt Design Group, Austin, Texas; Daimon Doyle, president, Doyle Custom Homes Inc., Olympia, Washington; Robert Kaiser, president, New England Institute for Management Inc., Cape Cod, Massachusetts; Terance Manly, design studio manager, Winmark Homes, Swannee, Georgia; Chris McDonald, co-owner and vice president of The Artisans' Group, Olympia, Washington; Peter G. Merrill, president and chief executive officer, Construction Dispute Resolution Services, LLC, Santa Fe, New Mexico; Kristen Nillsen, co-president, Gold Medallion Homes, Salt Lake City, Utah; Gretchen Palmer, co-owner, Palmer Homes, Bend, Oregon; and Dennis Webb, vice president of operations, Fulton Homes, Tempe, Arizona.

About the Authors

Gina Gullo and Angela Rinaldi are consultants to the building and design industries. Their company, Better Builder Strategies, offers services in design center option program development and implementation, sales and design training, operational organization, and space planning.

A business owner and operator for 30 years, Ms. Gullo has worked in retail, in the financial markets, and as an interior designer. She directed design studio development for WCI Communities Inc., a major home building and development company in southwest Florida, overseeing option programs, studio environments, operations, and training programs.

Ms. Rinaldi's experience encompasses 32 years in the education, retail, and home building industries. Her home design and option selection experience spans the high-end custom and production home markets. She has coordinated design development for custom homes, assisting discerning buyers one on one with the selection process. She helped manage a high-volume home design center and was the senior design associate and head of training for WCI Communities Inc. Prior to that, Ms. Rinaldi worked in publishing and advertising in New York.

In *Option Selling for Profit*, Ms. Gullo and Ms. Rinaldi share their hands-on understanding of high-powered selling in the ever-expanding market of options for new homes. To learn more about the services that Ms. Gullo and Ms. Rinaldi can offer to builders, visit their Web site at www.betterbuilder strategies.com.

Introduction

"Give me the luxuries of life and I will willingly do without the necessities."

– Frank Lloyd Wright

After seeing their neighbor's house, home owners commonly will remark that they didn't know that a particular feature was available and that had their home builder told them about it, they would have purchased the option for their home. Could this be 10% of your customers? 30%? 50%? Can you even guess? Even if it is only a small minority of customers, profit is profit. Many builders have found that in tough markets, option sales are adding significantly to their bottom line, generating 5 to 25% of revenue.[1]

Helping customers create a home that reflects their personal vision and individual style is the goal of option sales. A house is a shelter, but a home is a reflection of the owner. As such, it embodies the owner's lifestyle, tastes, hopes, and dreams. Therefore, once customers settle on their ideal location and preferred floor plan, the next step is choosing the optional home features and finishing touches that reflect who they are and what they want. By adding the features they choose, home buyers can customize even the most basic floor plan. They walk away happy because they have made the right choices and they know they are getting what they truly want in their new home.

In today's market you must appeal to customers' emotions and inspire their confidence. Creating an outstanding program of option choices, presented in a well-organized design center backed by a well-trained sales and construction team, will provide the competitive edge you need.

Unfortunately, what should be a fun part of home construction—for customers and builders—is fraught with potential for missteps. With all of the advances in home design, customers still commonly make remarks like, "Oh, don't buy it from the builder, the products are overpriced and it is much cheaper to do it after closing." From a builder's perspective, it's better to hear them say, "I was able to design my new home just how I imagined it to be! My builder had great products to choose from and good prices. We were able to roll everything into our mortgage payments and move in to a completely finished home." An exciting option program with established business practices and trained design and production teams will lay the groundwork for getting this kind of customer referral.

With a professional option sales program, builders—even in a down market—have reaped healthy profits by improving their processes for selling optional features and upgrades. Arizona-based Fulton Homes, for example, was able to consolidate design operations and streamline the design appointment for customers, contributing to a 61% boost in income from option sales.[2]

Without a professional system for selling options, customers are likely to feel hurried, ill informed, overwhelmed, and wary of buying what you are selling. An organized, individualized option sales program, on the other hand, allows a builder to uncover details about market preferences and helps build customers' emotional attachment to their new homes. When customers feel this emotional connection, they buy. Therefore, a professional approach to selling options lays the groundwork for dramatic increases in profits.

This book assists home builders in creating an effective and efficient option sales program by addressing the following:

- key elements for developing a valuable option program that appeals to your market
- steps to a well-organized and professional design appointment that better serves your customer and reduces the time spent selecting options
- effective techniques for better understanding and selling to the needs of your customers
- methods and tools for a well-run selections operation

The book also gives you access to a Web page with 19 downloadable forms and other tools that will help you create a well-run design center or reorganize your existing one to be more efficient and profitable.

Developing an option program does not have to be a burdensome process. It just requires prelaunch commitment to research, planning, organization, and teamwork. Customers depend on your company's expertise to deliver the home of their dreams. They look to you as professionals to guide them through the appropriate choices to satisfy their lifestyle and budget and to introduce them to new products they would not have discovered on their own.

Don't let profit slip through your fingers. Make the commitment now to create a well-organized option program that

- responds to your market's desires
- speaks in customer friendly language
- creates a rewarding home design experience for you and your customers

Option Selling for Profit explains in detail the techniques for serving customers better and helps builders and design professionals understand individual purchasing styles, learn what consumers value by actively listening to what they say (both verbally and nonverbally), sell concepts rather than products, and provide superior customer service.

When you successfully apply these strategies to make a customer's dream home a reality, you create satisfied buyers and referrals that will grow your profits.

What You Will Find on the Web page

The companion Web page includes the following tools:

1. Designer Commission Report
2. Candidate Assessment
3. New Hire Orientation and Training Outline
4. Sample Options Contract
5. Cover Letter for Mailing Options Contract
6. Profit and Loss Statement

7a. Designer Annual Business Plan–Part I

7b. Designer Annual Business Plan–Part 2

8. Design Center Department Report
9. Welcome Letter
10. Design Center Description
11. Option Selection Process
12. Materials Disclaimer
13. Design Center Appointment Preparation
14. Design Appointment Options Checklist
15. Active Customer Report
16. Customer Contact and Community Information Sheet
17. Record of Customer Correspondence
18. Contract Information Cover Sheet
19. Customer Survey

The files can be customized easily to meet your business needs. To access the files go to www.nahb.org/5xZQwery.

1

Housing and Paying for an Option Sales Program

There are three choices for housing an option sales program:

- building or leasing your own showroom to display options
- using your model homes
- outsourcing through an existing design center or other outlet

Building or Leasing Your Own Showroom

Owning or running your own design center is the most expensive alternative for displaying your option products, as it involves building construction or leasing and shell design, as well as display design and installation. If you choose this route, following are three possible alternatives to help you get started:

- **Hire a design firm that specializes in option showroom design.** These firms typically charge $5–$10 per sq. ft. At $10 per sq. ft., the design firm provides complete floor plan design, blueprints, all paint color detail, cabinet designs, and elevations. It also selects coordinating products, including countertops, faucets, tile designs, and lighting. This full-service design approach requires the least hands-on effort from builders. For an additional fee, the design firm will send a representative to oversee construction of the design space. At $5 per sq. ft., the design firm typically provides floor plan layout, blueprints, and color selection detail. The design display and product detail remain the builder's responsibility.

- **Work with your trade vendors to help design your showroom space.** Although a viable option, this approach requires more effort and attention on the builder's part. Manufacturers and contractors, especially larger companies, employ in-house designers. Therefore, look to your trade partners for assistance in designing individual areas such as kitchen, bath, home theater, lighting, and electronics displays.
- **Use a combination of professional design firm and trade partner support.** This is probably the most cost-efficient and effective method of designing your showroom, as it relies on experienced input while addressing budget restrictions. Contract with an expert for shell design and product display placement (kitchen area, bath vignette, home theater, etc.), color detail, and overall image. Again, look to trade partners to help design individual areas; they can choose cabinet elevations, create bath vignettes, and suggest coordinating products.

Starting Small

Builder-owned design centers aren't just for high-production builders. Even if your niche is one-of-a-kind custom homes and remodeling, you probably can do a better job of serving your clients and expand profit potential by bringing product selections together under one roof.

The Artisans Group Inc. of Olympia, Washington, which has been helping clients create one-of-a-kind custom homes and renovations since 1997, recently consolidated and expanded its operations to include a retail design center. The 1,000 sq. ft. center, in its second year of operation, was expected to bring in roughly a third of the company's overall design sales revenue.

The design center opened in 2006 as a service to The Artisans Group's custom home and remodeling clients. It was a logical approach to better serve customers. "We thought, wouldn't it be nice if our customers could come in and get the royal treatment?" says The Artisans Group's Co-Owner and Vice President Chris McDonald. "For years, we sent clients to multiple places to make their selections. Now we have most of it in one place; it's almost a one-stop shop. For plumbing and appliances they have to go elsewhere, but almost everything else they can select and purchase right here," he says. The center offers cabinetry, flooring, countertops, and tile.

The Artisans Group's design center sells products not only to its own design and construction clients, but also to other builders, builders' clients, and the general public, including do-it-yourselfers.[3]

Model Homes as Design Centers

An alternative to housing a design center in a centralized facility is using a model home to highlight options and conduct design appointments. Properly planned and executed, this option can be as effective as a full-service design center, especially when enhanced with technology. Because model homes already serve the function of showcasing a builder's floor plan and craftsmanship, why not take the cost-effective path to selling options and upgrades by making the model home a design center as well? Outfitting a model with a variety of available option packages allows your sales and design team to sell the floor plan and the interior packages in one environment. This piques interest in options from the outset, generates emotional connection, and helps customers visualize a product's use and function. Look to your trade contractors for product and labor contributions.

For example, Gold Medallion Homes of Salt Lake City, Utah, located multiple design centers in the finished basements of its model homes prior to opening a 1,200 sq. ft. centralized center in its new office building. Because the company likes to control the options process as much as possible, ultimately the owners hope to bring all options sales in house, says Gold Medallion Co–President Kristen Nillsen.[4]

Model homes offer the following benefits as design centers:

- They are cost–efficient.
- Options are displayed in "real–life" settings.
- They are an appealing environment that creates an emotional attachment to products.

This approach is best for builders in slow housing markets or builders who, because they appeal to a narrower market segment, might see less foot traffic through their models. If you anticipate high traffic or plan to reach a broader market, then a model home is not the best location for your design center. A better choice would be a separate design center, whether it is your own or one operated by a third party. Just as you would if you were creating a separate design center, work with your trade partners on product installation and with designers to create attractive spaces in your model homes. Most important, no matter where your center is, tailor your option packages and product displays to your targeted market.

Professional Designers or Merchandisers

Having model homes designed and decorated by professional merchandisers or interior design firms lends credibility to your home building company, especially if those homes are going to serve as design centers as well. While the expertise of professional merchandisers and interior design firms overlap in many areas, it is important to note one primary difference. Professional merchandisers have a greater concern for designing a space that generates the most revenue per sq. ft.; interior design firms are focused on creating well-appointed designs that create a wow factor. Following are some pointers for working with a merchandiser or design firm to stage your model homes:

- Determine the budget. Generally, builders allow a set amount of money per sq. ft. for design and options. For example, $40 per sq. ft. would allow $80,000 for a 2,000 sq. ft. home. This amount includes both product and the designer's fee for services.
- Clearly communicate to the design firm that options displayed should include both standard items and upgrades.
- Stress the importance of showcasing options that are salable and affordable to the target market. Desirable options that are overpriced or bargain-priced outdated options are a turn off to the customer and create a negative image for your company. Use your sales reports and work closely with the design firm or merchandiser in identifying the products that appeal to your home buyers.
- Ensure that the sales and design staffs are well versed in what options your company actually offers and which ones are design firm exclusives. The design firm exclusives are designs that will help customers remember your homes but they are not meant for resale in the option package program. Customers can be disappointed if they get their heart set on an option they viewed in the model and then are told that it is not available.
- Attractively frame a detailed list of the available option packages and post them in your model homes. To avoid creating unrealistic expectations and unhappy customers, clearly identify the items in the model that were created by the design firm and are not available for resale.

Working with Manufacturers and Trades

Whether a builder uses a model home or another location to house a design center, manufacturers offer an array of tools to help distributors sell their products. Catalogs, selection guides, and sell sheets are standard, but a growing number also offer more sophisticated tools, including upgrade calculators and design software on dedicated Web pages for construction professionals. Some offer custom quote programs that help dealers respond to customer inquiries promptly. Manufacturers also will provide product displays—even an entire kitchen or bath vignette—for no charge or a minimal charge if you agree to sell their products.

In addition, local contractors will offer reduced rates for installing products in your showroom in exchange for business from your home building company. They may expect you to sign a "contract for services" to guarantee them future work from your company. Whether you are negotiating with a manufacturer or another trade partner, an exclusive or nonexclusive contract may be employed.

In an exclusive contract, builder ABC agrees to sell, for example, a company's appliance products exclusively and agrees that no other company's appliances will be part of the builder's option program. Typically, this type of agreement includes a "standard" product for homes, as well as upgrade options. A nonexclusive agreement allows builders to sell products in the same category from multiple manufacturers or distributors. For example, a builder may

What Product Vendors Will Provide

- dealer pricing
- custom quotes and customized options programs
- design and planning software
- precrafted displays and product installation
- comprehensive training about products
- customized online product showrooms
- market research
- design departments to assist with showroom/display design
- Web portals and newsletters for construction professionals to share strategies and solutions

sell multiple countertop lines. Clearly, a builder has greater negotiating power with a manufacturer or distributor, and therefore garners greater financial benefit, from an exclusive contract because the product vendor is guaranteed greater sales. However, sometimes other business concerns take precedence over signing an exclusive agreement. For example, a builder in multiple markets may need a wider selection of product categories than is available from a single source.

Strive to incorporate the following into contracts with your product vendors:

Home Technology: Finding the Right Contractor

Nine out of 10 builders in a recent survey said that adding home technology to their list of options for home buyers increased or helped them stabilize revenue.[5] Electronic systems contractors (ESCs) are the go-to experts for planning and installing home technology options in your homes. Their specialties range from high-end to basic security installation and electrical contracting. In between, there are ESCs who specialize in planning and installation of home technology for mid-market, custom, semi-custom, and production home builders.[6]

- One-year minimum term of agreement. In certain market conditions, such as when prices are rising and product demand is high, builders can benefit from a two-year term.
- Price protection for the duration of the agreement. If this is not possible, at least negotiate a maximum allowable percentage price increase.
- Warranty coverage for the term of the agreement.
- Complimentary product displays for the design center. For agreements with trades that provide a service, such as installation, explain that the potential benefit to them is more jobs.
- A discount for products installed in model homes.
- Rebates based on annual sales to the builder. The amount varies, so negotiate these individually with your suppliers and trades.

Outsourcing an Options Program

When neither having their own design center nor a model home is a feasible alternative for selling options, builders can contract with a third party to handle option sales. The third party can be one of the following:

- independent design center with additional revenue interests
- independent design center that specializes in builder option sales
- interior design firm experienced in merchandising model homes

A third-party design center with additional revenue interests is typically a medium-to-large manufacturer, installer, or retailer that provides a service to builders that may eventually create opportunities for revenues in another segment of the third party's business. For example, the third party design center sells and installs flooring as well as operating a showroom, and is interested in developing business relationships with builders. You can expect involvement and assistance from the third-party design center in developing your option program—a benefit to builders who are novices in option sales. Ask your flooring and cabinetry suppliers if they offer this service.

A third-party design center specializing in builder option sales is a design center available only to builders for their customers' use. Its main function is conducting option appointments and offering design services to the building industry. As with the previous alternative, the design center will assist the builder in option program development. The builder does not have to purchase products in order to use the center for option appointments; a longstanding partnership may involve only the design appointment transaction.

An interior design firm with merchandising experience is a design firm with its own design studio and experienced designers who are also salespeople. Its primary business is residential or commercial design. These firms provide excellent partnership opportunities for small local builders.

One Size Doesn't Fit All

Gretchen Palmer, co-owner of Palmer Homes of Bend, Oregon, founded in 1977, says best practices as well as housing cycles have influenced how the company has marketed and sold options. Although Palmer Homes began by selling options in its model homes, finish selections were outsourced to a local flooring company. The home builder later abandoned the approach because buyers were being shown a more extensive array of options than Palmer had agreed to offer and home buyers were waiting days to learn options prices from the third party. Meanwhile, home buyers were visiting big-box stores to get prices and then arguing with Palmer Homes' representatives about option costs. Eventually, the home builder brought all option sales, including finish selections, in house. The company created a design center in its office building, complete with cabinets, door styles, plumbing fixtures, lighting, tile, carpet, hardwood flooring, and accent wall colors.

When the company downsized, it still maintained control of the options program, but relocated displays to a room in one of its model homes. Palmer Homes also demonstrates various options in other for-sale homes. "Our buyers appreciate the range of choices, the ease of choosing prepriced selections, and dealing with only one person—our community representative who knows the options and what is or isn't possible at what stage of construction. We will never outsource our options to a third party again," Ms. Palmer said.[7]

For other builders, using independent design centers has proven to be a profitable choice. Regardless of which route you choose in selling options, develop an arrangement that specifically suits your market and your business model.

Compensation

There are three options for compensating a third-party design center: flat fee, commission, and purchase or exchange agreement. You may employ only one of these or you may use a combination of them.

Under a flat-fee arrangement, the third-party design center and the builder cooperatively schedule design appointments with customers. The builder pays the design center a flat fee for each appointment. This fee is based on the volume of homes constructed each year, average home price, and number of appointments permitted per customer. Fees typically range from $200 to $300, depending on your local market, for a three- to four-hour appointment. The builder pays the design center monthly, following the month in which the appointment occurs.

Under a commission arrangement, the builder pays the designer at the design center a commission, based on a predetermined rate. Commission rates range from 1 to 2% and are based on the builder's projections of annual option sales. Graduating commission rates is a popular practice because it provides an incentive for the designer to sell upgrades and help customers create a home that represents their lifestyle. For example, the builder may pay 1% on options sold up to a predetermined dollar amount and 1.5% for all option sales that exceed that amount. Some builders base the commission paid on the category of option sold; the builder may offer the designer an added incentive for selling a product category that realizes greater profit margins.

Finding the Best Alternative for Your Company

The type of organization you select for your design center appointments depends upon what is available in your area, the level of assistance your program requires, and your company's marketing image. The best avenues for researching your available opportunities for the option selection appointment include

- the Internet
- builder and option magazines
- builders shows
- NAHB 20 Clubs
- local home builders associations

A builder or design center manager can use tool 1, the Designer Commission Report (fig. 1), to track option sales and commissions by month and for the year to date. The report is an Excel spreadsheet organized by customer, dollar amount, and if applicable, option category. Compile the report as follows:

1. Insert the current year, designer's name, and month.
2. Input customer name, community name, floor plan, and lot number.
3. Key in the total value of options in dollars, as shown on the options contract.
4. Place an "x" in the appropriate column indicating commission percentage. The spreadsheet will calculate the commission amount in the "Total Commission" column. The "Adjustment" and "Final Commission" columns are for manual calculations, if needed.
5. Have the designer review his or her commission reports.

FIGURE 1 Designer commission report (tool 1)

Year: __________

Designer/salesperson: ____________________

Sales for the month of: ________________

Customer	Community	Floor plan	Lot #	Total option sales	0.75%	1.00%	1.50%	Total commission	Adjustment
Squire	Chelsea	Bella	24	$30,000.00	x			$225.00	
Squire	Chelsea	Bella	24	$18,000.00	x			$135.00	
Squire - change order	Chelsea	Bella	24	($2,000.00)	x			($15.00)	
McNulty	Nob Hill	Estate	2	$75,000.00		x		$750.00	
Anderson	Larkspur Lakes	Terra	17	$8,500.00	x			$63.75	
McNulty-change order	Nob Hill	Estate	2	$5,000.00		x		$50.00	

The builder receives a copy of the spreadsheet monthly. In turn, the builder submits a monthly closing report to the design center. For invoicing, this statement is compared with the center's appointment schedule. The center then calculates the commissions owed for the month and invoices the builder.

Purchase or Exchange Agreements

Under a purchase or exchange agreement, the third-party design center's compensation is an agreement that the builder will purchase products or services from the third party. For example, ABC Builder uses the design center for its option selection appointments. Rather than agreeing to a flat fee or commission payment, ABC Builder agrees to use the third-party design center's flooring installation service for a year. Another alternative could be that ABC Builder agrees to purchase all of its flooring from the third-party design center. In this scenario, the designer is paid by the builder, not the third party.

Tips for Partnering

The following guidelines will help you incorporate a third-party design center into your option sales program and create a customer-focused design center environment:

- **Comparison shop.** Get at least three bids to ensure that you are getting the best deal for your money, but beware of making a decision based solely on price.
- **Make it easy to buy.** Look for a center with clean and attractive product displays. Overwhelming customers with too much visual stimuli hampers their decision making.
- **Find a good match.** Seek out a design center with an image that is compatible with your company's, paying attention to how its employees dress, as well as the overall appearance of the center itself. This will reinforce for the customer that they are working with a company that promotes their lifestyle.
- **Brand it.** Confirm that your company's brand and logo are well represented in the design center. Your name should be visible wherever your customer is purchasing product. This will reinforce your brand with the customer.
- **Don't rush customers.** Ensure that the center has quiet areas for customers to take breaks during their

selections appointments and to discuss privately when there is an impasse on selections. This can reduce anxiety and save time by allowing customers to overcome disagreements and move toward a purchase.

- **Be child friendly.** Look for children's rooms separate from the appointment areas. The selection process can be a long and boring one for children, who are naturally active and curious. Providing a place for them to play or watch a movie will keep children occupied while their parents purchase products.
- **Establish preview hours.** Be sure the center has preview hours for customers to view products prior to their design appointments. This will save time at the appointment because customers will have had a chance to weigh and discuss option choices ahead of time.
- **Respect customers' time.** Ensure the center has flexible hours that allow customers to make appointments in the evenings and/or on at least one weekend day to accommodate working customers' schedules.
- **Make a connection.** Clearly communicate that the designer represents you as well as the design center. Again, this will reinforce your brand and help the designer earn your clients' trust.
- **Develop an exit strategy.** Establish a protocol for canceling option contracts. Negotiating in advance the compensation to be paid in the event of a canceled contract will help the builder–design center relationship.
- **Price products right.** Ensure that items are priced per room or area and in packages because this is the most effective way to present and sell products.

Building the Design Team

Regardless of which route you choose in developing an option sales program, understand that the design team is critical to making a program work. Moreover, a customer will evaluate their home buying experience based largely on the design center process. Therefore, don't underestimate its importance to your home building company's overall reputation for customer service.

Virtual Design Center

You may be tempted to pursue having an entirely virtual design center; however, this is not the best option. Color is not duplicated well in photos or online. Products such as flooring, cabinetry, and countertops, which have color variations, or products whose primary feature is their color, are best viewed in person. The best scenario for a design center is a combination of virtual and real-life product viewing with guided assistance from professionals.

Designer/Sales Consultant

Although all positions are important in running an effective and productive design center, the designer/salesperson on the front line with the customer is the person who will leave the customer with either a positive or a negative impression. In addition to having people skills, they must understand the building process, interior design, and human psychology.[8]

Table 1 shows the winning attributes of a design center salesperson and the relative importance of each characteristic.

Although sales prowess is paramount, design ability, time management, and organizational skills are important as well. Seek out designers who have a proven history of working with multiple clients simultaneously. Inquire about their tracking and filing systems. Ask for examples of how they kept track of their clients and their follow-up techniques. Finally, seek candidates with three to five years of sales experience with one company. Longevity is often an indicator of a good track record in sales.

If after the first interview you have a candidate who has proven sales and design experience or a candidate who does not have a sales background but has interviewed very well, schedule a two-part Candidate Assessment (tool 2). The assessment lasts 1 1/2 to 2 hours and is given at the second interview. Part I is a 15-minute written test that measures an applicant's presentation, sales, design, and technical knowledge. Part II is a sample design presentation. The applicant gets 60–75 minutes to select materi-

TABLE 1 Winning attributes of a design center salesperson

Attribute	Essential	Very Important	Important
Proven sales experience	●		
Organizational skills	●		
Verbal skills		●	
Written skills		●	
Industry knowledge			●
Strategic thinking ability	●		
Computer skills		●	
Outgoing			●
Time management skills	●		
Appearance and attire			●
Design ability		●	
Retail background		●	
Multitasking skills	●		
Team oriented		●	

als and then 15–25 minutes to make a design presentation to the design center manager and an experienced designer as though the candidate were in an actual customer appointment. Use the evaluation checklist at the end of the test to rate the applicant's presentation and selling skills. This checklist can be used later in determining the training schedule for the new employee.

Design Center Salesperson Compensation

There are two options for compensating option salespeople: flat salary and base plus commission.

In a flat-salary program, compensation focuses primarily on the designer providing customer support, guidance, and information throughout the design center experience. The salesperson's primary concern is providing service rather than up selling options to the customer. Salaries range from $40,000 to $70,000 annually, depending on the market, home prices, number of available options, salesperson experience, and number of customer appointments per year. A metropolitan area with a higher cost of living in a high-end community with an extensive option package program would compensate the designer closer to $70,000. Some in the industry believe that the flat-salary system is good for customer service and supports a noncompetitive environment among design center salespeople. However, this system also encourages extended appointment times and stagnant revenues.

Base-plus-commission programs tie incentives and commission percentages paid to the total dollar amount of options sold. For example, sales associates might earn a base salary of $25,000 to $35,000 depending on their experience, plus commissions of 0.75 to 1.5%, depending on the total dollar amount of options sold. Builders using this type of system realize greater option sales and customer appointments are streamlined for efficiency. In addition, this approach increases customer satisfaction because options are packaged and sold as a total lifestyle concept that suits the individual customer. However, if you choose this option, make sure that your salespeople are not sacrificing customer service to increase sales. Your interview process and training program should leave no doubt in a candidate's mind that your ultimate goal is superior customer service and customer satisfaction.

Training

A strong training program will increase motivation and problem-solving skills among staff and increase productivity and profitability in your option program. Manufacturers offer product-specific training that includes information on benefits, care, warranty, and upgrade options. In addition, builders or their third-party design centers should have their own internal training program. "We invest in our designers with hands-on and video training programs," says Dennis Webb, vice president of operations for Fulton Homes of Tempe, Arizona, which increased option sales by 33% in one year through a retail selling approach.

Design sales professionals also need competent staff to support their efforts, so cross train nonselling design center staff members in the design center to ensure consistent customer service during vacation periods. Also include these staff members in product and sales training meetings and seminars. Enroll the receptionist and other employees in e-mail and telephone etiquette training.

Tool 3, New Hire Orientation and Training Outline, is a two-week training schedule for new design center employees. Your management team can use it to guide training of new designers and salespeople. The first- and second-day schedules may be used to train support staff as well.

Remember that design center staff is your company's billboard. Make sure they are telegraphing a positive message!

Build a Product Training 'Library'

A good practice is to invite each of your trade partners to provide a monthly one-hour training session about their products. These sessions can help improve sales at the design center through increased product knowledge, including installation and warranty practices. Your sales, construction, and purchasing personnel all can benefit from this training.

File materials from each training session into a 3 to 5 in. heavy-duty binder. Label the binder with the manufacturer name and the month and year of the training session. Update the material annually.

Other Key Positions

In addition to sales staff, there are four other design center positions. Your company's size will determine whether you fill some or all of these positions.

1. Design center manager. This individual is responsible for overall performance of the center and its sales,

budget performance, and employee training. The manager is the liaison to other departments and maintains constant communication and flow of information with the purchasing, construction, sales, closing, warranty, and, if applicable, architectural departments.

2. Design center operations manager. This manager is responsible for the options and option packages. This person also works closely with the purchasing department, facilitating ongoing communication and information exchange. In addition, the operations manager works with trade contractors to maintain the design center's option products and assists the manager in employee training, including arranging training seminars conducted by trade partners.
3. Receptionist. This person greets customers, answers telephone calls, schedules design appointments, facilitates daily design center activities, and maintains the customer database and related files.
4. Design assistant. This entry-level employee supports sales staff in managing design center customers. The assistant should be trained and ready to assume a design sales position within six months to a year. Design assistants gain product, design, and sales knowledge by working closely with designers.

2

Thinking Like a Retailer

The design center concept of one-stop shopping for options and upgrades was created by builders to survive a housing slump in the 1980s. They began offering home customization under one roof in an effort to boost business and lure new customers. Rather than asking customers to drive from showroom to showroom selecting flooring, cabinets, appliances, faucets, and other features, as was customary, builders began to bring all of their products to one location. Some of these design centers are now builder owned and on-site at a community, or they may be at separate locations and outsourced.

Although design center revenue is now estimated to be as much as $20 billion annually, some builders continue to overlook this vital portion of their business interests.[9] Too often option sales are an afterthought and a design center is considered to be more work than it is worth. But to the contrary, a well-run design center can generate profit that exceeds builders' expectations. For customers, these centers can take the home buying process to a higher level by offering lifestyle customization with retail flair. It's like giving customers that extra bit of chrome on the motorcycle or the perfect pair of shoes!

Indeed, the automobile, furniture, clothing, and electronics industries include many examples of companies that capture buyer loyalty by gearing their marketing and advertising to appeal to consumer lifestyle. A prospective automobile customer visits the Volvo dealer for a new car because he or she is looking for a clean, uncluttered design that emphasizes safety. This customer profile is likely to have a classic style of dress, minimal interest in impressing others, a social conscience, and a no-fuss approach to life. The IKEA furniture customer, while also being concerned with function, may be independent, free-spirited, and artistic as well.

Flourishing retail companies master the art of lifestyle marketing through advertising an image that customers identify with or want to be part of because that is how most of us make purchase decisions. Although we buy because we need or want something, a particular product's characteristics make us choose one company's product over another's. Offering an option program that aligns with your customer's interests means creating an environment for them to recognize and then purchase the product that reflects their unique lifestyle.

Along with lifestyle marketing, the following key ingredients of any successful retail operation can be applied to option selling:

- **Train your employees.** Well-trained, knowledgeable, and professional employees let your customers know that you want them to have a positive experience with your company. Employees represent your brand through every phase of the transaction, so be sure that they do it well. Teach them how to create loyal, happy customers who enjoy doing business with your company. When a company invests in its employees, it is rewarded with better customer service. Southwest Airlines, for example, has focused on creating a fun working environment for employees because company executives realized that if employees were happy they would pass their enthusiasm on to customers.

- **Humanize your company.** Use your employees and customers in your advertising, marketing and Web sites. Seeing real employees in advertising promotes feelings of trust and familiarity with prospective customers.
- **Price products competitively.** Today's consumers are perceptive and well educated. They are aware of the latest trends and the newest styles. They are acutely conscious of what things cost and where to find the best price. They have information readily available to them via TV, the Internet, and magazines. Customers know when they are being taken advantage of with exorbitant prices and they don't like it. Nothing will break down trust and confidence in a consumer like the realization that they are overpaying. They will feel like they have been lied to, which is not a path to a good relationship.
- **Diversify for growth potential.** Even when home sales are lagging, builders can maximize the value of every purchase by invigorating their option program. A well-designed option program with new and innovative prod ucts that are appealing to a particular market segment will enhance the customer experience and build profit.

Dennis Webb credits Fulton Homes' retail approach for its design center's success. In one year, the company increased option sales from 12% to 18% of base home price. Fulton set a goal of becoming more customer focused with its design center operations. The company then developed an online catalog, using a readily available commercial program. Fulton revamps design center displays to keep pace with customer demand.

On the pricing side, Mr. Webb attributes the success of the option sales program to one important factor. "We take realistic markups because our customers are smart and have many resources to check pricing. Markup is determined by sales, not purchasing." To ensure the company operates its design center space profitably, Fulton Homes determines the amount of product sold per sq. ft. of design center space. The company establishes sales goals for each option category and targets specific areas for improving sales. Fulton Homes also brings in experts where needed, such as in the structured wiring and home theater areas. "We continuously address the customer experience by being technologically advanced in the design and sales centers," Mr. Webb says.

To succeed as a retailer, you will need to put yourself in the customer's position. Successful retailers ensure that their processes are communicated well and with consistency, product descriptions are succinct, price lists are available and complete, and employees follow up with customers.

In other words, as a retailer you must create systems that will improve the customer experience and buyer satisfaction. What would you want to hear if someone were talking about your company's vision, goals, mission, practices, and products, unaware that you were listening? Ideally, your option sales should support that declaration.

As a retailer, you need to be flexible. Before closing his store for the night, James Cash Penney, founder of JC Penney, would walk outside and look up and down the street to be sure he wasn't shutting out potential customers. As long as there were customers to serve, his doors stayed open. You don't have to operate 24/7, but you should be responsive to customers. The customer is a priceless treasure. Be sure to align your systems, service, and products accordingly.

Streamline your product offerings and gear them specifically to your customers' tastes and needs. Package options to eliminate overwhelming a customer with hundreds of choices. Give the packages personality by naming them, such as, "wired package," "super wired package," and "extreme wired package," representing three levels of connectivity; or, "steely D solo," "steely D duo," or "steely D trio" for three levels of stainless steel appliance packages. Be as creative as you like; give the products personality and your customers will respond.

Another key to retail success is to keep communication lines open between salespeople, who interact daily with customers, and managers and executives who create company programs and systems. Frontline staff is an invaluable source of information about the end users of your product and how to serve these customers better.

Successful retailers capitalize on consumer desire to express who they are in what they buy and own. Builders who approach options sales as retailers have an opportunity to outsell their competition. Remember, referrals and repeat business only come from satisfied customers.

Marketing a Design Center

According to Chris McDonald of the Artisans Group, marketing is an ongoing challenge. His company had been known primarily for architectural design, drafting, and construction services prior to entering the world of interior design and retailing. With so many diverse interests, "the challenge is explaining [to customers] what we do and how we can help." The core of The Artisans Group's design center clients is the top 20% of customers who are more service- than price-oriented when they make home and interior design purchases. "Some professionals in the home building industry have expressed surprise that we're expanding in a down market, but I say, 'Think of who we're expanding to,' " Mr. McDonald says.[10]

Promote your design center as one-stop shopping that brings all available option products to your customers in the comfort of a professionally designed showroom. This eliminates their having to spend countless exhausting hours visiting showroom after showroom of products. Your design center is a valuable marketing tool for your company. It offers your customers a complimentary, personalized design service when they purchase a home from you. Play up and advertise that you provide this complimentary design service because, typically, interior design firms charge considerable fees for this expertise. Market your design center—on your Web site, in your model homes, and in the design center itself—with the message: "Come visit our professional, experienced design consultants who are trained to help you create the finished home of your dreams."

Don't Forget Parade of Homes

Most local home builders associations sponsor a Parade of Homes each year, and in some areas, vendors offer builders a 10 to 30% discount on materials that will be used in participating homes. Builders can potentially save buyers several thousand dollars by timing a home completion to the parade of homes. Check with area suppliers to see if these types of discounts are available to boost your home and option sales. Green materials, in particular, are likely to be popular attractions in future parades of homes.[11]

Using the Home Sales Center

The home sales center is a wonderful venue for promoting your design center. Prominently display photographs of it in your sales center and model homes. You can also display sample boards of various option packages to help customers visualize how they could customize their home. These boards should be roughly 18 × 24 in. and professionally matted and framed. A whole-house package board would include, for example, the following samples, scaled to the amount of material used in a particular room or space:

- flooring
- cabinet finish
- countertop
- appliance and fixture finishes
- bath tile
- decorative tile

Complementary fabrics could be shown to enhance the palette.

Your company's Web site also is a natural place to promote your design center. Create a tab specifically for the center, with information about its products and processes. Introductory text could state, for example

> "Welcome to our design center, your path to customizing your home to suit your taste and lifestyle.

> We provide you the opportunity to create your dream home by adding products that reflect the latest trends and contemporary needs of today's home buyers. We invite you to browse our design center and review our product offerings. Call us for more information."

Your design center Web page could include

- photos of the design center and its employees
- testimonials from satisfied customers
- examples of popular options with descriptions and a few photos such as a theater room, kitchen vignette, and an outdoor kitchen
- a simple, interactive design tool that allows visitors to experiment with cabinet and wall finishes, flooring and countertop materials, and appliance colors

Present your design center as a benefit to your customer. Clearly explain the design service, emphasizing how your design professionals can help customers coordinate design, color, texture, and mood, while contributing to their new home's resale value.

Inside the Design Center

Your design center's ambience should reflect your company's style, personality, and the homes that you build. For example, Winmark Homes in Swannee, Georgia, re-created a traditional American main street as the stage set for its design center. To reinforce that the company is family owned and to promote small-town ambience, "shops" within the design center were named after different family members in the business. Design center customers could stroll from storefront to storefront to select various options and upgrades for their new home. These boutique-like settings proved to be fun for customers and productive for the design center. In a two-year period, option revenue increased by 30%.

"The design concept has been extremely successful. Our customers love it. They even bring friends back to enjoy it with them," says Terance Manly, Winmark's design center manager. "With so many option choices, our customers feel like they are building a custom home even though we are a production builder and they purchased a production home. They feel good about that!"[12]

KB Home employed an entirely different but equally effective approach to option sales. The company placed its model urban homes against a lighted cityscape. Each model was merchandised with different option packages designed to appeal to various targeted markets. Each package contained specific standard selections with limited upgrades. In general, buyers responded by spending 10% of a home's base price to personalize their homes.[13]

Space Functionality

When considering function, examine your space, determine how your customers will move through it, and plan accordingly. Create a design center that will guide the customer smoothly and efficiently through the product selection appointment. Train new hires on how to process customers—both home buyers and other prospects—from sales through the design center process as illustrated in chapter 4.

Include appointment areas that are intimate, uncluttered, and relaxing. These areas don't need to be enclosed offices, but they should provide privacy and reduce distractions. At the same time, keeping appointment areas somewhat open to the surrounding environment of product displays will help energize and excite customers about possibilities in their new homes. Think about how you gravitate toward where the action is when shopping in a mall or visiting the International Builders' Show. You are curious about what others are hearing about, seeing demonstrated, or buying.

Create efficient and effective desk space for the designer, either on the design floor or in a back office. The designers' desks should be off the selling floor, even if you must place them in a shared office space. Each designer's desk should

- be in a cubicle for privacy and noise reduction
- be L or U shaped, depending upon space allowance, for plan review
- have a two-drawer file cabinet
- have a shelf for product catalogs and information

The common office space should include file cabinets that house completed customer files until after closing, a copier and scanner, bookcases for training material, and cabinet space for sample product storage. If the designer desk space is small because of limited back-office space, incorporate a counter-height table 5 to 6 ft. long and 2½ to 3 ft. deep. For convenience, the table can be hinged, with foldable legs, so that when it is not in use it can be tucked away against a wall.

If your showroom is small or you are using a model home that does not allow separate office space for your design center, you can still create functional office space on the display floor or in a model home. For example, a built-in office alcove in the kitchen, or in a third or fourth bedroom, could be used, as could an office armoire located in a family room. Simply create a shared area, away from customer traffic, to accommodate samples, customer folders, and training material.

Product Displays

Even with the explosion of online purchasing, consumers still like to see and touch product samples before they buy. Creating real-life displays in your design center allows your customers to envision the possibilities of their new home. Moreover, customers frequently purchase what they see on display. The customer sees, wants, and buys. When customers can actually experience products, they become more enthusiastic and excited about them, especially when the products are electronic, such as a home technology or lighting package. Following are a few examples of displays that appeal to the emotions of customers.

Home Theater

Most studios have a reception area where customers can wait for their designer to greet them. What a great opportunity to create a memorable display of a desirable option package! This is a perfect location to create a home theatre room, with a large-screen TV, surround sound, stereo, special lighting, and an automated control panel.

Kitchen

Kitchen designs are another popular and profitable display. The kitchen should be professionally designed, color coordinated, and incorporate working appliances, including specialty items such as wine coolers, trash compactors, and steam ovens. It should include upgraded cabinets and countertops with a coordinated decorative backsplash. The sinks and faucets should follow the design style and possibly include an island with a sink and fixtures with custom high-end finishes such as hammered copper. Spend a few dollars on accessories that add to a lived-in feeling, such as a basket of artificial fruit, ceramic cookie jar, or decorative serving platters.

Master Bath

The master bath offers another excellent opportunity to appeal to customer desires. Elegant, luxurious, master baths are synonymous with fine living. Create one with a small air tub, steam shower, designer sinks, and faucets. Make it even more special and inviting with a lovely floor medallion or glass tub skirt. Light the toe kick of the cabinet and include a silent exhaust fan. Better yet, install a disappearing TV in the vanity mirror!

In fact, a clever and successful retail strategy for gaining customer attention and creating excitement is to incorporate a few unusual products throughout the showroom. Even if most customers do not purchase the high-end products, these features will catch their eye and draw them to the displays. Once there, the designer can discuss other available options.

Use the following guidelines to create product displays that will win buyers over.

- Show the "included" or "standard" products. Customers feel cheated if they move from display to display and are unable to see what is included in the home. Be sure to display your standard (included) products such as
    - bathroom sink, faucet, cabinet, and countertop
    - flooring, including carpet, tile, and wood
    - kitchen cabinets
- Allow visibility and floor space proportionate to the profit a product generates. For example, invest more space in cabinetry display than in trim molding display.
- Limit choices within categories and/or price ranges to six or fewer. Studies have shown that offering too many choices overwhelms customers and hampers their decision making, resulting in fewer sales.
- Allow customers to interact with products. A great interactive option, used by a design center in southwest Florida, was a wireless automated lighting option. Several lighting modes were programmed into the system and multiple styles of working lighting fixtures demonstrated each. Customers were able to press buttons to view various options. For example, "morning mode" included the island light and under-cabinet lighting illuminated; "entertainment mode" was pendant lights and spotlights illuminated; and "good-night mode" was a single low-lit light.
- Create sample boards that show a complete design concept for a specific area, (think HGTV design shows). Use these boards as props during an appointment to help a customer visualize the finished product. For example, a master bath design board could include the shower tile, floor tile, and decorative tile accents. These predesigned concept boards are time-savers. They offer

design solutions that appeal to a customer's lifestyle and eliminate tedious efforts in selecting individual products to achieve the same look.

Regularly integrate new products into your established displays. Don't leave new samples on the floor, in a corner, or leaning against your existing displays. Impress your customers with your attention to detail and convey the value of product displays. Be sure all showroom products are correctly identified and labeled.

View your design center as an opportunity to impress customers with your company's professionalism and to showcase the best products in home design. The most successful option programs create an environment that, like any pleasing retail store, makes it easy for a customer to buy. The goal is to lower the customer's defense against buying, and make them eager to select your products to create a home that reflects their individual tastes and lifestyle. The following recommendations can help you ensure that your design center is customer-centric:

- Continually review all products on display for currency and availability. Don't set customers up for disappointment by displaying products that are no longer available.
- Mount professional quality photographs of your finished homes or model homes and place them throughout the design center. These pictures not only represent your image to the customer, they display your

Fashion Forward that Won't Break the Bank

Changing your design center displays can be a costly endeavor, but there are ways to minimize cost and still display current products. For example, the cabinets, countertops, and flooring comprise most of the cost in a kitchen display; therefore, select traditional styles with a longer shelf life. Then, create excitement with trendier products such as backsplashes, island cabinets and countertop, lighting, and faucets. Finally, work with designers and salespeople to identify what customers want. If the product isn't selling and the display looks tired, then it is time for a change.

current option packages and provide another platform for promoting lifestyle design.

- Invest in technology, such as virtual design programs, to help customers view how their selections will work together. (Design center technology is discussed in more detail in chapter 3.)
- Be customer friendly and avoid overly complex procedures. Create easy-to-read and easy-to-understand product style descriptions and price lists.
- Keep your design center clean, clutter free, and organized.

Virtual Showrooms

Virtual showrooms are design center tools that allow customers to see on a computer screen or television screen how their option choices will look in a room. Use at least a 32 in. flat-screen TV for best results. Imagine a counter-height workstation, approximately 36 in. deep by 48 in. wide, with comfortable seating for customers and a hydraulic pop-up TV. Take the work station a step further with a locking cabinet for your customers' personal belongings, a drawer for designers' appointment tools, and a light.

Another application for virtual showrooms is to incorporate them in your Web portal for customers. Allowing customers to experiment with various floor, wall, and cabinet finish combinations in the privacy of their homes can help them narrow their preferences prior to the design appointment. This tool can help customers make selections in advance. It can also generate excitement about the upcoming design appointment.

Virtual showrooms support package selling. For example, you can show a kitchen or bath design and the upgraded option items within a package. An upgraded kitchen package might replace the free-standing range with a built-in microwave and oven combination, use cherry raised-panel cabinets instead of oak flat-panel cabinets, include stainless steel instead of white appliances, and add a cooktop and decorative exhaust hood. Showing the look on a large screen makes selling the upgrades easier.

3

Managing for Greater Option Profit

Revenues grow when options are presented in ways that excite customers and lead them to purchase additional products. A well-planned program anticipates and mitigates potential problems, reduces costs associated with selling options, and creates satisfied customers. The following guidelines will help you avoid common errors in product selection, presentation, and pricing, and achieve success with an option sales program.

First, you should identify your market niche or the group of customers that you want to serve. Understand what your customers are purchasing, and then develop an option program that fits their profile. A successful option program does not try to offer every conceivable product. Instead, it aligns products with a targeted market.

Work with product vendors to create your option program. They can alert you to best sellers, past installation difficulties, and potential warranty problems. In addition, they will assist you in creating the option packages.

Be sure to price options competitively. If products are overpriced, they will not sell. Do not charge more than your market will bear, and do not give your margin to your subcontractors. Although a 60% margin may be desirable, if a markup prices your customers out of an option, they won't buy it. It may be advantageous to lower margins and sell to more customers. Remember, zero sales on a product with a 60% margin equals zero revenue.

Package your option offerings into complementary groups and categories. This not only helps your customers with decision making, it can help you price the products competitively and still allow you to make your margin.

Ensure that products you are displaying are available. A cumbersome chain of events occurs when a customer has chosen a product that is no longer available. The designer then must call the customer, find a replacement product, and reissue paperwork, frustrating the customer and, possibly, delaying construction.

Make sure you know the installation costs in advance. Just because a product is in high demand doesn't mean that it will adapt well to your construction processes. Be sure that installation costs are in line with your profit goals for your option program.

Keep your product offerings up to date. Locate and feature options that customers want and remove outdated products from your offerings. A design center full of products that your customers do not want will not generate revenue. It also reflects badly on your company. Therefore, create a system and designate a person to review, maintain, and incorporate current market trends into your option offerings.

You should be knowledgeable about product trends. Ask for recommendations from your design and sales staff about what to offer, as they are the closest to the customer. Read trade and consumer magazines for insight on product trends. Find out which products other builders are offering and make your program competitive with theirs. This up-front planning will save time and money in the future. The International Builders' Show and kitchen and bath shows provide excellent opportunities to view new products and gather information on hot-selling items. When attending these shows, use your time effectively by visiting new vendors and limiting time with those you already know. Your purpose is to find new products, get fresh information, and connect with more people. Take time prior to the shows to review the exhibit floor plan and organize your path to minimize walking time.

Organizing your product inventory is one of the most important steps to a successful selling program. Investing in an online option catalog can help you stay organized. The benefits of online catalogs far outweigh the minimal cost of setting one up. Your can organize your option products by category, package, item, price, and color. Some photos and product descriptions can be uploaded directly from the manufacturer to your online catalog. If your current product offerings are well organized, with accurate style and model numbers, migrating them to an online catalog should be a breeze. However, if your current offerings are scattered and disorganized, the transition will be more difficult.

Ensure that your staff is knowledgeable about the options being offered. In addition to selling techniques, they should understand installation procedures and timelines. For example, when selling a steam shower, the designer must be aware that the option involves having other options installed at various construction stages. Therefore, it is important for the designer not to sell the steam shower after a certain point in construction. Providing ongoing product training helps ensure that your staff is well informed.

Develop a computer-generated options contract, allowing space for options selected, changes, and special instructions. Handwritten notes are unprofessional and can be difficult to read, creating problems in the field. Tool 4 (fig. 2) is a Microsoft® Excel-based Options Contract. Your designer can input information directly into the contract to create a professional document to give to the customer. A copy of the Options Contract also should be maintained in the customer folder.

FIGURE 2 Sample options contract (tool 4)

Sample Options Contract						
Company Name						
Date: March 17, 2008					**Floor Plan:** Bella	
Client: Squire, Jim and Susan					**Unit/Lot Number:** 24	
Salesperson/Designer: Sara					**Area:** Chelsea	
ITEM #	**OPTION #**	**LEVEL**	**ROOM/ZONE**	**OPTION STYLE/MODEL #**	**OPTION DESCRIPTION**	**COLOR / FINISH**
1	**ELEVATION--EXTERIOR**					
2			Elevation	A	Bella Plan	
3			Exterior	Paint Colors	Ivory with Slate Trim	Color Scheme #3
4	E12345		Roof	Tile	Shaker Style	Charcoal
5	**SUMMER KITCHEN**					
[illegible]	[illegible]	2	Patio	Vendor ABC Style #1122	Electric Grill Model 31-inch - 120 Volt Electric Grill	[illegible]

Pricing

With the Internet and television shows devoted to home products, today's consumers are inundated with new product information. Seeing the range of choices available, consumers want the latest styles at a price they can afford. You will be well positioned if you can offer them value-added expertise about products as well as fair prices. If you price your products right, you can increase sales volume and make more money. On the other hand, exorbitant prices set up a sales scenario of uneasiness and distrust. Once a customer believes that the pricing is unjustifiable, it is very difficult to rebuild their confidence in your business.

Packaging Options

Combining or grouping products into packages (fig. 3) assists customers with their selections and makes design appointments efficient and profitable. Sell key packages that appeal to your customer's tastes and lifestyle, rather than offering an array of disparate products. The luxury and green packages discussed later in this chapter are examples of lifestyle packages. Offer all packages at three price levels of good, better, and best.

M/I Homes of Tampa, Florida, generated nearly $200,000 in additional options revenue in one year by embracing increased demand for home technology. The builder worked with an electronic systems contractor, S&S Electric of Oldsmar, Florida, to design option packages that would appeal to most home buyers in its Easton Park community. "By not completely customizing each home, we were able to maintain strict production schedules and provide product options that were profitable for us and M/I Homes," says Lisa Turbeville, vice president of sales and marketing for M/I Homes.[14]

Following are some advantages of selling options as packages:

- high profit margins because of the ability to negotiate package pricing
- fewer field issues as predevelopment of packages allows time for contractors to be adequately trained to properly install components
- control over the number of option choices, so customers are not overwhelmed with selections
- reduction of customer's cost concerns because they are purchasing a group of items, rather than focusing on individual item pricing
- increased perception of value in the consumer's mind as packages are designed and presented by knowledgeable professionals

Sample Option Packages

Following are generic examples of option packages. As with housing plans and elevations, these should be designed, labeled, and priced to appeal to particular housing market segments.

Lighting

This package offers upgraded lighting in selected locations, plus one additional location of the customer's choice as follows:

Preparing the Options Contract

Prior to the customer's option selection appointment, the designer creates an electronic customer folder with the Options Contract and other electronic documentation. The electronic version of the Options Contract can be referenced for years after your paper documentation has been archived.

This electronic folder should be housed in the community's master electronic folder. Label the customer folder with the lot or unit number, customer last name, and floor plan (in that order) and paste a blank Options Contract into the folder. Do not change the worksheet tab name from "options contract" unless the contract is a change order.

To label the contract, open it, then click "view" and "header and footer" on the toolbar. Click "custom header" and input the community name. *Do not change* the center or right-hand sections of the header or the footer; these are preset to output the contract with the customer name you have created, current date, page of pages, and initials line. After closing the header, input the customer's name and other specific information in the contract.

After the customer makes their selections, the designer inputs the options information into the contract, along with prices, and prints out the contract. The customer signs the contract and returns it with a deposit. The signed hard copy goes in the customer folder, which is explained in more detail in chapter 7.

An expanded, more advanced version of the sample (BBS Option Contract System) combines the option pricing spreadsheet with the Options Contract and, through computer filtering, imports the pricing spreadsheet into the Options Contract. More sophisticated contracts are available as part of packaged information technology (IT) solutions for option selling.

If you need to mail the options contract to your customer, you can use the Cover Letter for Mailing Options Contract template (tool 5). The letter should be printed on your company's letterhead. Send the letter with the option contract and a self-addressed overnight envelope. Upon receipt, the customer reviews the contract, signs it, and returns it with a deposit check.

- foyer
- dining room
- bathrooms
- additional light location, per plan

Kitchen

This package offers upgrades to appliances and other popular kitchen features as follows:

- appliances (e.g. French door refrigerator 25 cu. ft. model number ___, 30 in. electric cooktop model number ___, 30 in. built-in microwave/wall oven combination model number ___, and extra quiet dishwasher model number ___).
- sink and faucet
- countertop
- cabinets
- backsplash

Luxury

This is a detail package that includes decorator and information-age upgrades such as

- crown molding in living room, dining room, and master bedroom
- computer, security, television, and telephone wiring
- interior paint
- master bedroom closet organizer

Green

This package allows builders to respond to the growing consumer demand for energy-saving and green-building practices with the following options:

- low-energy windows
- water recycling system
- water-cooled air conditioning
- passive solar water heating
- whole house water purification

Other packages can be designed for specialty rooms, such as wine, spa, and game rooms.

Whole House

Design style distinguishes whole-house packages, in which interior elements work together to form a unified whole reflecting a particular style direction. The direction may be traditional, contemporary, or eclectic. In terms of options, each package includes a few choices of countertops, flooring materials, cabinet colors and styles, and other finish items. After extensive market research, Toll Brothers began offering traditional, transitional, and contemporary whole-house packages to eliminate buyer guesswork.[15]

A contemporary package might include the following:

- stainless steel appliances
- quartz countertop with coordinating tile backsplash
- sleek sink and faucet designs
- maple flat-panel cabinets
- bamboo flooring
- low-pile carpet
- polished chrome bath fixtures
- white contemporary bath fixtures
- large wet tile in bathrooms

FIGURE 3 Examples of option packages

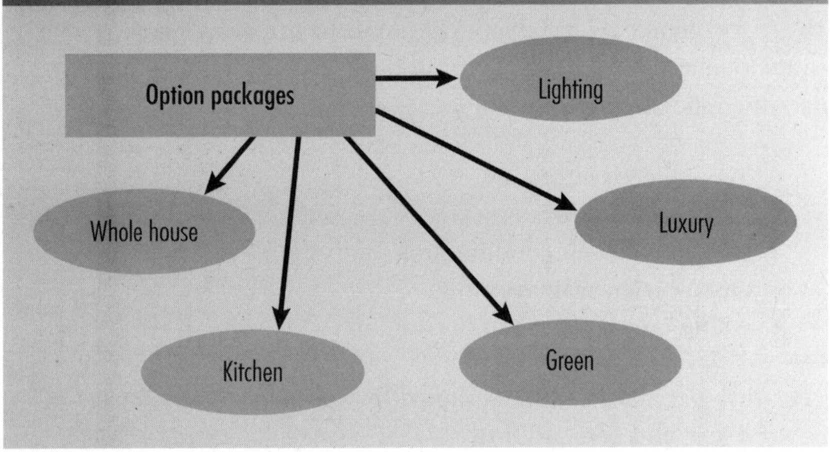

Regardless of what packages are included in an option program, they must appeal to a range of style preferences and they must include the following product details:

- accurate model numbers
- color detail
- complementary design and style within each package

Once you become familiar with product offerings, competitors' packages, and design styles, package pricing can be applied to wide array of products beyond the preceding examples. By developing well-designed packages, you can improve pricing and margin controls, streamline the design center appointment, create a platform for lifestyle selling, and simplify your inventory maintenance.

Although option packages are key to time efficiency and profitability, some customers still wish to select options à la carte. Therefore, balancing your option program with packages and à la carte items will offer the best scenario for generating revenue and creating the highest level of customer satisfaction.

Goal Setting for Option Sales

The most successful builders in option selling take time to set goals and create an option budget. Option sales are measured as a percentage of the base price of the home. A good benchmark is 8 to 12%, but work with your managers and other key personnel in home sales, the design center, and finance to create realistic option sales goals. Incorporate incentives to encourage them to get to higher percentages.

For example, builder ABC plans to construct and close 200 homes in the upcoming fiscal year. The builder's average home price is $400,000 which would result in $80 million in annual budgeted revenue from home sales. Builder ABC, with input from key managers, decides on $6.4 million for the option sales budget for the year, (200 homes × $400,000 = $80 million × 8%). The annual goal is then divided into monthly goals, with adjustments to reflect higher- and lower-traffic months.

Measuring Progress

A monthly Profit and Loss Statement, which is tool 6 (fig. 4), can help you measure progress and stay focused on the goal. It's best to do a quarterly analysis because high-dollar purchases involve a longer decision-making period and may skew monthly predictions. Quarterly analysis recognizes the typically longer time frame for large purchase transactions.

FIGURE 4 Profit and loss statement (tool 6)

Company Name
Design Center
Profit and Loss Statement
For Period Ending: [Month]

Opt sales month actual	% of opt sales	Opt sales month plan	%	Variance FAV/(UNF)	Description	Opt sales YTD actual	%	Opt sales YTD plan	%
$900,000	100.0%	$850,000	105.9%	$50,000	Gross design options*	$900,000	100.0%	$850,000	105.9%
$525,000	58.3%	$485,000	57.1%	($40,000)	Cost of goods sold*	$525,000	58.3%	$485,000	57.1%
$375,000	41.7%	$365,000	42.9%	$10,000	Gross profit	$375,000	41.7%	$365,000	42.9%

Expenses month actual		Expenses month plan		Variance FAV/(UNF)	DC operating expenses:**	Expenses YTD actual		Expenses YTD plan	
$29,200		$25,000		($4,200)	Designer selling expenses	$29,200		$25,000	
$23,400		$25,000		$1,600	Administrative expenses	$23,400		$25,000	
$9,400		$10,000		$600	Occupancy expenses	$9,400		$10,000	
$62,000		$60,000		($2,000)	Total operating expenses	$62,000		$60,000	
$313,000		$305,000		$12,000	Operating profit/(loss)	$313,000		$305,000	
					Other income				
					Other expenses				

Design center sales goals should correlate with the monthly option sales budget. For example, let's assume the monthly design center option sales budget for January through March is $500,000 (January), $500,000 (February), and $1,000,000 (March), and that three designers are selling options. The monthly sales goals for each designer would be approximately $170,000, $170,000, and $335,000. The design center manager works with the designers/salespeople to achieve the goals.

The Designer Annual Business Plan (tools 7A and 7B) shown in figure 5 allows you to track the previous, current year, and planned sales for each designer. Using this sales-enhancing tool, the design center manager works jointly with designers to create annual business plans for each designer selling to customers. The manager and designer finalize the business plan for the upcoming year during the last two weeks of the current year. Both individuals keep a copy. Creating these business plans ensures that the design center and designers strive to grow option sales year after year to meet company expectations. Working together in creating these business plans garners designer commitment to the goals because they feel management supports their efforts. Each step of the plan builds upon the previous one, beginning with a review of the previous year's performance. Fulfillment of the plan depends on monthly coaching. The plan is useful in conducting performance appraisals for salary increases or bonuses.

FIGURE 5 Designer annual business plan (tool 7B)

Designer Annual Business Plan—Part II **Name:** **Year:**

	Actual Sales $ (previous year)	Option %	Planned Sales $ (insert this year)	Option %	Actual Sales $ (insert this year)	Option %	Comments
JAN	$ 159,000.00	6.0%	$ 170,000.00	8.0%	$ 187,000.00	10.0%	Excellent Quarter!
FEB	$ 159,000.00	8.0%	$ 170,000.00	9.5%	$ 155,000.00	10.0%	Great consistency in your
MAR	$ 316,000.00	10.0%	$ 335,000.00	12.0%	$ 375,000.00	14.0%	option %, with a banner
Quarter	$ 634,000	8.0%	$ 675,000	9.8%	$ 717,000	11.3%	third month! Good job!
APR	$ 325,000.00	9.0%	$ 345,000.00	11.0%	$ 359,000.00	12.0%	Nice start to the quarter.
MAY	$ 215,000.00	8.0%	$ 228,000.00	10.0%	$ 215,000.00	13.5%	Great Month!!
JUN	$ 160,000.00	7.0%	$ 170,000.00	10.0%	$ -	7.0%	
	700,000	8.0%	$ 743,000	10.3%	$ 634,000		

Business Planning

The design center manager uses the business plan as a template for determining each designer's strategies and option sales goals for the upcoming year. The result is a comprehensive plan for increasing design center revenue by improving product knowledge, designer business systems, and design talent.

The plan is developed jointly by the design center manager and the designer/salesperson prior to the next fiscal year. Begin with an analysis of the previous year's performance to highlight achievements and build upon strengths. This positive approach and two-way discussion between manager and designer is key to encouraging the designer to overcome weaknesses and implement the business plan. The design center manager should plan 90 to 120 minutes with each designer to create the business plan.

The annual business plan is developed to maximize the five-stage design center sales cycle. Brief explanations of the five stages follow:

1. **Making customer contact**—sending an orientation packet to the customer and following up with a telephone call
2. **Gathering information**—getting to know the customer prior to their design appointment
3. **Providing service**—conducting the design appointment
4. **Gaining customer commitment**—closing the sale, reviewing paperwork, and securing customer signature and deposit
5. **Following Up**—providing customer service

The design center manager works with the designer to identify the designers' strengths and weaknesses and to develop strategies to improve performance. Chapters 5–7 offer in-depth guidance for handling each of the five stages well.

A business plan conversation between a manager and designer might proceed as follows:

> MANAGER: Last year you achieved $1,350,000 in option sales, with an average option percentage of 9% of base home price. You worked with 50 customers who purchased homes with an average price of $300,000. This year, if you were to increase

> the percentage to 11%, you would increase your option sales to $1,650,000 ($300,000 × 11% × 50 homes). That is a one-year increase of $300,000 in option sales. At 1.5% incentive commission you would earn an additional $4,500. Achieving this goal for the upcoming year would involve selling each of your 50 customers an additional $6,000 in option product. Do you believe you could achieve this new goal?
>
> DESIGNER: I think so; $6,000 more to each customer does not seem like a large amount of money. All I would need to do is sell an outdoor kitchen option or upgrade the main area flooring. I am fairly good at suggesting new product to my customers, but sometimes not very good at overcoming their objections, even though I believe the suggested product would benefit them. Could you help me improve my skills in this area?
>
> MANAGER: Absolutely! Let's set up a time to role play so I can demonstrate a few different scenarios for overcoming objections. In addition, I will speak with Katie about working with you. She is our top-producing designer and sells options worth 15% of the home base price on average. How does that sound?
>
> DESIGNER: Great! I think that will really help me increase my sales. Thanks for your help.

Now that is a great scenario: a happy salesperson, excited about selling more, and a manager who has just set the stage for increasing design center annual sales by $300,000 with just one designer! By implementing the designer annual business plan with strategies to improve product knowledge, business systems, and creative talent you could be on your way to a more profitable design center.

After the manager and designer have agreed on the upcoming year's option sales goals and dollar amounts, actual sales can be tracked, month by month, and compared with the previous year's results. As a team, review the business plan and spreadsheet in monthly meetings to assess whether goals are being met and discuss plans to improve, if necessary.

Sales Tracking

To ensure that your packages are desirable, you must stay abreast of trends and continually monitor whether customers are selecting or declining a particular package. Therefore, developing tools for tracking the sales rate for particular option products is vital to increase option profit. Customer surveys are one method to gather feedback on the success of your option program. In addition, as part of their services, online catalog companies provide a multitude of reporting options for analyzing your option sales. Your vendors and trade partners can help you track sales as well.

Because they work with a variety of builders and remodelers, trade partners can clue you in to consumer preferences and best-selling products. They also keep reports on your best-selling products. Manufacturers, especially larger companies, have sophisticated programs for analyzing sales and tracking information as well. They track sales by item, company, month, and year. Your vendor contact commonly will provide you with the information from these reports. Use them to evaluate the popularity of your current product offerings.

Information Technology

Home builders on the cutting edge of option sales have found IT tools can help them manage the burgeoning array of design features and upgrades. These tools run the gamut from online catalogs to comprehensive option-selling solutions. Technology solutions can help you improve your own efficiency in options sales.

Online Catalogs

Web-based option catalogs are an affordable tool to help manage products. Builders have three choices for populating product information—automatically, manually, or a combination of both. Online catalogs

- Boost a company's image, professionalism, and Web presence.
- Help educate customers about product features and guide design center sales staff about customer interests and preferences.
- Help educate the design center staff about product features and specifications.
- Allow product manufacturers to submit product information directly to the online program, including customer friendly marketing material and color photos.
- Maximize design center appointment time and streamline selection processes by allowing customers to preview option choices prior to their appointment. Designers can view their customers' product preferences, use these and information gained in the preappointment telephone call to focus the appointment on desired products, and suggest additional products.
- Enhance the customer experience. Customers can preview products in the comfort and privacy of their own homes, without feeling pressured. Couples can discuss important design elements and product preferences prior to the design appointment, and they can save preferred choices to a wish list.

Administrative Tools

"In any business, the backbone is process mapping and systems development," says Mr. McDonald of The Artisans Group. "Where does this piece of paper go? Who needs what? Who's going to bill the client?" Information technology can assist you with managing option contracts, controlling paperwork, and making communication easier. Following are just a few examples:

- Storing customer contracts in an electronic system with key word search functionality can reduce the time needed to locate customers who may be impacted by a product substitution and notify them of the change.
- Scanning option contracts, customer change orders, photos of products, diagrams, pricing backup, and notes related to the option selection process can help eliminate boxes and boxes of archival files.
- Using voice recognition software instead of pencil and paper can save hours of transcribing notes from telephone conversations and composing e-mails to recap conversations.

More complex technology solutions for selling options help actively manage customers. Besides capturing sales prospects, these programs actually develop packages, offer virtual showrooms, include architectural support such as blueprint design assistance, and tie into back-office functions that support field operations, purchasing, and billing. When properly implemented, these tools can help you save time and money and provide long-term process improvements that will increase customer satisfaction.

Technology solutions are not a silver bullet though; they require a committed effort to link systems and train users for maximum efficiency.

Reporting Tools

Fulton Homes officials take full advantage of information technology to analyze rates of sale and markup. They then can determine what products to offer and how to price them based on hard data. For example, "if the figures tell us we are selling more bathroom sinks, we bring in more styles of sinks," says Mr. Webb.

Off-the-shelf IT solutions provide the following tools for reporting and analyzing results:

- **revenue analysis**—reports by category, date, and current versus previous periods
- **rate of sale report**—a ranking of options in order of best- to worst-sellers and percentages of customers purchasing specific options
- **margin report**—earnings and labor costs per option
- **sales report by designer**—individual designers' sales by dollar amount, category, and options sold to each customer as a percent of a home's base price

Look for the following in selecting electronic tools to employ in your option sales program:

- ability to upload a specific floor plan and design each room using products designated for that floor plan
- consistent placement of options into logical product categories
- a place for detailed product information alongside the option, such as model number, colors, and details written in plain language for the customer
- easy access to information for updating, adding or eliminating products, gathering customer-specific information, and analyzing data
- a smart, user-friendly search tool that helps locate products and information quickly
- a program that follows your design center's process, rather than an accounting program retrofitted to use in the option selection process

Inventory Control

Creating an automated option selection process demands inventory consolidation and organization. If the option inventory is unorganized—with outdated model numbers and information—

then your system becomes ineffective. In other words, garbage in, garbage out. Use IT implementation as an opportunity to

- clean up your inventory
- create consistent reports
- discover top-selling options and eliminate bottom sellers
- reduce errors
- increase product consistency
- improve profitability

Design center software program prices vary widely according to their functionality, flexibility, and customization. Therefore, before investing in technology, ensure that your design center operation is systemized, organized, and structured to offer up-to-date products and superior customer service. Then, determine whether the IT programs you are considering will do the following:

- generate customer friendly option contracts
- provide reports for analyzing profit margins and rates of sale for specific periods
- allow easy product management
- incorporate ongoing training and support
- meet the demands of your current business and plans for future growth

No matter how large or small you choose to make your options program, seek out avenues to automate it. Research software companies and select IT solutions that meet your individual needs.

Design Center Department Report

Tool 8, the Design Center Department Report (fig. 6) tracks the option contract and related information for each customer who visits the design center. It serves multiple purposes, including tracking sales performance of designers and status of customer selections. It is useful for determining whether option contracts are completed and processed within your company's established time frame. For example, your company might set a standard that customers will have their first design appointment by 30 days after signing the home sales contract and that the option contract will be completed no later than 30 days after that first appointment.

FIGURE 6 Design center department report (tool 8)

Tool	8																
								Design Center Department Report									
Community Name																	
Closed date	Constr. stage	Lot #/Unit #	Neighborhood	Floor plan	Elevation	Contract date	Customer Name	Sales Initials	Designer Name	Design appt date	Base home price	Lot premium amount	Structural options amount	Design option contract	Change order #1	Change order #2	Total design options
		2	Nob Hill	Estate	B	02/09/08	McNulty	BB	Sara	02/15/08	$500,000			$75,000	$5,000		$ 80,000
																	$ -
																	$ -
																	$ -
																	$ -
																	$ -
																	$ -
																	$ -
																	$ -
																	$ -
																	$ -

In addition, the report can track option sales as a percentage of the base price of each home. Finally, it may be used as a sorting tool for information on individual designer sales revenue. Although the report is maintained by one person, many people may have access to it. Use the report to track all option contract and related information for each customer who visits the design center and to evaluate the percentage of option dollars generated by each home owner.

Following are some tips for using the design center department report template:

- Format the report to print landscape on 11 × 14 in. paper.
- The "closed date" is the month and year that the home owner closed on the home.
- The "contract date" heading is designated for the home contract, not the option contract.

- The "option % of base home price" is the dollar amount of options as a percentage of the base price. (Base price is the home price before adding lot premiums or structural option costs.)

The report is maintained either by the design center manager or the receptionist, who will input information as follows:

- Make the initial entry when the design center receives the home contract.
- Enter the customer's name, information about their home, and their design appointment date.
- After receiving the customer's deposit check, enter that amount.
- After the option contract is processed, enter the total option contract amount.
- Enter the contract closing date, which indicates that warranty phase has begun.

The option percent of base home price is calculated by dividing the total amount of options by the home's base price. The design center management uses the percentage as a measure of each designer's sales performance. Using the data/filter functions in Excel (in the arrow boxes at the top of each column) allows the manager to view the value of all of a particular designer's option contracts.

Allow other departments, such as purchasing, sales, construction, and property management to have viewing access to this report. Doing so will help keep everyone informed about the customer's option selection process.

4

Maximizing the Design Center Experience

To ensure that the customer's design appointment is as productive and stress free as possible, offer them multiple ways to learn about your company, options, and processes beforehand. Written, telephone, and face-to-face contact prior to the design appointment helps decrease common customer complaints of feeling confused, overwhelmed, and rushed in the buying process. When customers experience these emotions, they are in no mood to spend money on optional features. Therefore, orient customers to your processes with a packet that includes information about your option selection program. This is the first but not the last step in preparing them for a rewarding experience in the design center (fig. 7). Builders find that when they prepare buyers well for the design center appointment, customers are better able to make selections and apt to spend more money on options and upgrades.

For example, Winmark Homes' Web site allows customers to create a wish list of options before their appointment at the design center. The design consultant can review the list in preparation for the design appointment. In addition, the Web portal asks customers for personal information that helps the designer

FIGURE 7 Design center process for home buyer

- **Customer buys home**
  - **Community salesperson**
    - Faxes to design center:
      - customer contact sheet
      - sales contract & addenda
  - **Design center receptionist**
    - Confirms customer's design center appointment or schedules an appointment
    - Sends customer orientation packet
    - Creates hard copy customer folder
    - **Designer**
      - Creates electronic folder on customer
      - Contacts customer by phone
      - Prepares for design center appointment
      - Conducts design appointment using options checklist
      - Files signed options contract in customer folder
    - **Design center operations manager**
      - Processes option contract
      - Posts contract & related documents to shared network (or e-mails)
      - Logs information into Design Center Department Report

understand the customer's lifestyle. "This gives us an opportunity to get to know our customers' needs and desires before they reach the design center and customize a palette for their particular lifestyle," says Mr. Manly.[16] Similarly, a portal on Fulton Homes' Web site includes a review of the design center process for customers as well as a "style identifier quiz" to help them with option selections.

Orientation Packet

The orientation packet should include a Welcome Letter to customers (tool 9) the Design Center Description (tool 10), and a description of the option process (tool 11). The community salesperson may provide and explain the packet to customers at the home sales center or the design center receptionist can mail the packet to each customer, along with the designer's business card, after their home purchase and prior to the design center appointment. A more comprehensive packet also includes the following:

- design center location, hours, a map, and driving directions
- accepted payment methods
- brief design center staff biographies
- schedule for selecting options and deadlines for completing the option contract
- request for customer to commit to process and schedule
- request for customer input about what they like and don't like about their current home
- an option selection form for customer review
- disclaimers regarding materials and other issues (tool 12)
- answers to clients' frequently asked questions (see chapter 7)

Telephone Introduction

Not making personal contact with a customer prior to their design center appointment is akin to meeting them on a blind date. To avoid an awkward first meeting, design staff should call the customer prior to their first appointment to introduce themselves and to ensure that the customer has received (and read) the orientation packet. The telephone call offers an opportunity to begin a positive relationship with the customer, learn about their needs, and manage their expectations.

After a brief introduction, the design staff person should address the following items in the preappointment telephone call:

- Review the length of the appointment.
- Provide driving directions or alert the client that you will e-mail directions.
- Discuss the appointment procedures, target dates for the appointment, and option selection deadlines.
- Confirm customer contact information.
- Establish expectations for the option selection process.

Information Gathering

Of course, you will need more information about clients to assist them in making selections, including facts about their lifestyle, whether and how they entertain, preferred colors, design concepts they like, specific needs, and budget. You will ask questions to elicit this information and take written notes on their answers. Product vendors, such as cabinetry manufacturers, often have detailed questionnaires on their Web sites that you can download and pass along to your clients for this purpose. Following are suggestions for questions to ask customers during the preappointment telephone call:

Lifestyle

1. How would you characterize your style (traditional, casual, formal, casual elegance, contemporary, transitional, eclectic, country, uncluttered, cozy, lived-

in, welcoming, indestructible, functional, informal)? Select as many as apply.
2. Do you work from home?
3. What are your hobbies?
4. What do you enjoy most about your current home?
5. What do you enjoy least about your home?
6. Do you travel frequently?

- Color direction
  1. Do you prefer light or dark environments?
  2. Do you prefer jewel tones, pastels, or neutrals?
  3. Ask the customer to bring fabric and finish samples that represent their color preferences.
- Entertainment style
  1. Do you frequently entertain people in your home?
  2. How many people do you entertain?
  3. Are your gatherings casual or formal?
  4. What room do you usually entertain people in?
- Specific needs
  1. Do you have special design needs for your new home?
  2. How long do you plan to live in the home?
  3. Is it a part-time or full-time residence?
  4. Do you have pets?
- Budget
  1. Have you developed a budget for options?
  2. What are the primary rooms or areas where you would like to focus in adding options?
- Design concepts
  1. Ask the client to bring fabric samples and/or possessions that may inspire their options selections.
  2. Ask them to describe their preferred design styles.
  3. Discuss specialty items, if they are available through your design center, such as dishwasher or refrigerator drawers, cappuccino makers, specialty kitchen faucets, steam showers, and green products.

Following are some ways to approach budget with the client, and discuss upgrades and options as a percentage of the base home price:

- Eight percent of base price of the home allows some customization, such as upgraded flooring in certain areas, enhanced kitchen cabinets, and possibly kitchen or bath countertop upgrades.
- Fourteen percent allows greater customization, including all countertops, master bath decorative tile, and structured wiring of the home.
- Eighteen percent or more allows for full customization of the home to reflect the customer's personal taste and lifestyle.

Providing Service

The previously discussed steps to making contact with customers are designed to help you get to know them so you can serve their needs. After that they will have the opportunity to interact in person with you and your product line.

Product Preview

Use your Web-based catalog to allow customers to preview products prior to the option selection meetings. If you do not have an online catalog, you can schedule preview appointments at the design center. A design center employee should guide the preview meeting, which should not last more than one hour. These previews will reduce the time needed for customers to select options and are likely to encourage more purchases. In addition, offering opportunities for potential home buyers to browse your design center may be just the sales inducement they need. Figure 8 outlines the design center process for prospective home buyers.

FIGURE 8 Design center process for prospective home buyer

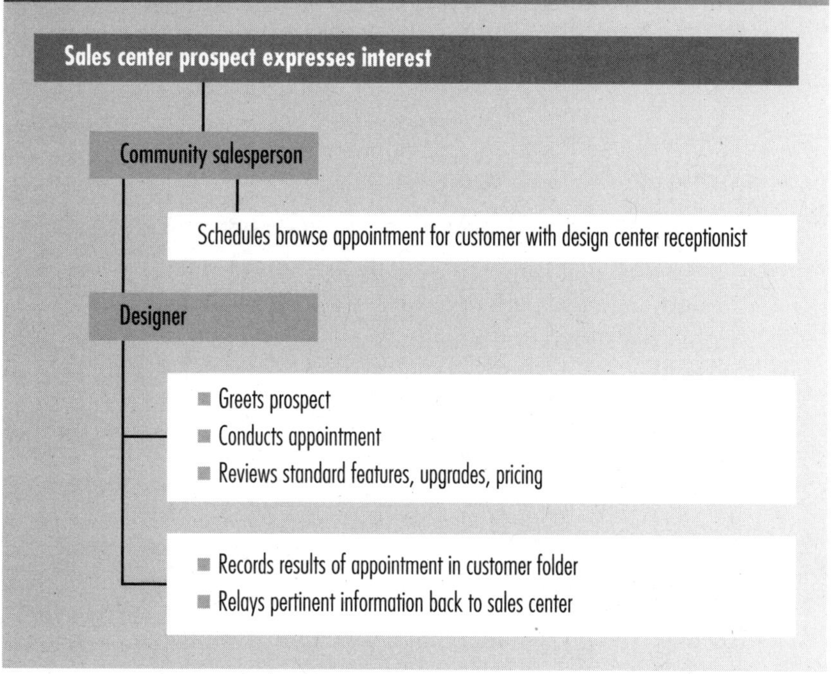

Preparing for the Appointment

Before the customer arrives at the appointment, set up the area where the designer will present the options and have the following items ready:

- diagrams and blueprints, if applicable
- pricing spreadsheets
- notes from previous conversations with the home buyer
- a toolbox including a tape measure, calculator, pens and pencils, ruler, and color samples
- design appointment options checklist
- customer folder with sales contract details, customer information, and home plan specifications

The Design Center Appointment Preparation document (tool 13) outlines procedures for preparing and organizing for a design center customer appointment. You can add this tool to your new hire training manual.

Conducting the Appointment

First impressions are everything and you only have one chance to make a memorable one. The customer's perception of the design center experience starts when they step through your front door. It continues with the designer's greeting and is fully established by the time they complete their appointment. It is essential that the interactions leading to and through the design appointment are systematically executed to ensure that your customer has a productive and enjoyable experience from beginning to end.

Approach the customer within minutes of their arrival and introduce yourself with a smile and a confident handshake. Walk them to the presentation area. Take time to converse with them before discussing business. Discuss how the appointment will proceed, offer them a beverage, ask if they are ready to begin, and when they are, start the presentation by reviewing the following with the customer:

- design appointment options checklist
- contact information
- notes from the preappointment telephone introduction conversation (to ensure that the information is still accurate and the customer has not changed their mind about style direction or other items)
- the home's floor plan
- deadlines for choosing options and completing paperwork
- outline of the process and next steps
- questions they may have

Reassure the customer that customizing their home with options will be positive and rewarding for them.

Present Design Options

The Design Appointment Options Checklist (tool 14) shown in figure 9 outlines option offerings by category and helps ensure that designers present all available options to the customer. You can customize this tool to reflect your option offerings and use the "Comments" section of the form to record options the customer specifically requests. At the conclusion of the options appointment, before a contract is finalized, the designer should ask the customer to sign the checklist. Keep a copy of the signed checklist in the customer's folder (behind the Record of Customer Correspondence) and give a copy to the customer.

FIGURE 9 Design appointment options checklist (tool 14)

Design Appointment Options Checklist

FRAMING ________

FLOORING
- Tile ________
- Tile on Diagonal ________
- Grout ________
- Floor Listello's Deco's, Medallions ________
- Carpet ________
- Padding ________

KITCHEN ________
- Cabinets ________
- Opt Cabinet Accessories ________
- Cabinet Hardware ________
- Countertop ________
- Countertop Edge ________
- Kitchen Sink & Faucet ________
- Opt Kitchen Backsplash ________
- Water Filtration Systems ________

LAUNDRY
- Cabinets ________
- Hardware ________
- Opts per Plan ________

INTERIOR PAINT COLORS ________
- Opt Two Tone Paint ________

ELECTRICAL ________
- Standard Plan ________
- Structured Wiring ________
- Opt Ceiling Fans ________
- Opt Decorative Lighting ________
- Opt Bath Lighting ________
- Opt Surge Protector ________
- Opt Intercom ________
- Security System ________
- Digital Thermostat ________
- HVAC Filters ________
- Music & Sound System ________

Following the design appointment options checklist builds a foundation for organization and control of the option selection process. It also helps present the selections in manageable bites so that a client does not become overwhelmed, as often happens. Although a designer is an experienced professional who works with different designs, finishes, and colors daily, the consumer is a novice and probably is viewing many products for the first time. By addressing selections step-by-step and gaining the customer's agreement along the way, customers are less apprehensive and more excited to see their new home (and significant investment) come together.

Help your customer see the home they are designing by displaying their palette as you build it. Begin by selecting a low-traffic area in the design center to create your customer's palette. Be sure you have a sturdy wall to prop selections against and favorable light. Start building the palette by laying the flooring selections and then continue with cabinet finish and hardware, followed by countertop selection and backsplash material, if applicable. Also add a sample selection for appliance finish (most appliance companies supply mini samples on key chains to design showrooms for just this purpose). Include a kitchen faucet sample and/or faucet finish selections. Group all kitchen selections together.

Build your bath palettes adjacent to the kitchen palette. Begin with master bath flooring and wet tile samples along with sink/commode/tub color and faucet sample and finish. Continue on to guest baths and laundry.

Be sure to group each room's selections together to create an accurate visual of the palette. In larger homes where the selections include many rooms, you will need to create multiple palettes.

Once the customer selects all options, take digital photographs of the completed palettes. Pictures become especially valuable six months down the road when memories start to fade. Organize photos with the product information and pricing and present them to the client in a professional and organized format. Use a folder that displays the home builder's name and logo to reinforce the brand.

Finally, review the necessary paperwork, answer any questions, and reassure the customer that you are available for follow-up. These steps ensure that customers will leave with a sense of accomplishment and with confidence that they are in good hands.

After-Contract Changes

If permitted at all, changes to an option agreement should be made within 30 days of the signed contract. If a change is made, the design center creates a change order which the customer signs, and secures a payment from the customer. A change order follows the same path as the original option contract for circulating the information. Rather than making the change order a separate document, the preferred method is to create a revised contract to supersede the original one. If you choose to use separate change orders, date and number them sequentially, and ensure the most recent information is reaching key departments in a timely manner.

Prior to closing, the designer should do a walk-through of the customer's new home with the most current option contract in hand to ensure all selections are installed. If there are errors, they can be remedied before the customer is invited to do their final walk-through.

5

Selling to Customers' Personalities and Values

Skilled salespeople working in a professional environment will regularly pull in over-the-top sales numbers, have the happiest customers, get the most referrals, and make it all look effortless. Although they may appear to have a golden touch, their steady stream of successes isn't mere luck or a magic formula. Lasting sales success originates from a deep desire to help customers and provide them with the best service, not being a fast talker or a "smooth operator" who quickly closes a sale, and then moves on to the next customer. While efficiency and effectiveness are important, they are only worthy when coupled with an honest desire to serve. Customers definitely notice the difference between being treated as the next number in line instead of a valued part of the company's success. When the latter is the desired outcome, the customer is a customer for life.

A good salesperson must balance personality with a sincere desire to provide good customer service. "If you oversell, you risk scaring the customer away," says Ms. Nilssen of Gold Medallion Homes.

"The salesperson's basic job is helping customers overcome their fears. The best way to start is by slowing down and really listening to your customers. People in the market these days are looking to you to reduce their uncertainty. Listen to them, reassure, and remind them that this can be the best time to make home purchases," says Ross Robbins, CSP, CMP, MIRM, of Lee Evans Group/Shinn Consulting.[17] Beyond that, we're going to let you in on the secret to a successful selling career: the ability to connect to and then sell to the customer's personal vision. In order to do this, all sales professionals, including those who are part of your design team, must

- know and understand the customer's personality type
- develop good listening skills and identify customer listening habits
- be conscious of the messages communicated through body language—both theirs and their customer's
- understand the customer's needs and values
- use suggestive selling to market a concept, not just a product
- understand and genuinely embrace the customer's concerns
- clearly explain the process and manage customer expectations
- go beyond the customer's expectations and provide excellent service

Knowing the Customer

There are four common personality profiles, and each exhibits specific buying behaviors. It is important to understand which one of these most reflects the customer sitting in front of you and why and how their profile makes purchasing decisions. Once you understand who your customer is, you can build an interactive information exchange with them that will help you fulfill their needs. For the salesperson, engaging a particular personality type is as crucial to success as properly targeted product advertisement. If a company does not accurately identify its target market, the product will be a flop. Similarly, if a salesperson does not accurately identify the customer's personality, they will not be able to engage, and ultimately sell to, the client. When personalities and communication styles are in conflict, the customer withdraws. The result is an uneasy customer, a frustrated salesperson, and low (or no) sales.

The STAR buying model identifies the four personality types as strong, talkative, apprehensive, and researcher. General guidelines for working with them are as follows:

Strong.	A talker who enjoys attention, this person also is a keen listener who wants to get everything in writing.
Talkative.	Always ahead of the process mentally, thinking of the next question, this person is not always listening to you. You will have to repeat yourself and gain agreement throughout the discussion.
Apprehensive.	To tap into the mind of this overthinker, you must ask high-gain questions that will clarify the customer's desires and ease their uncertainty. For example, you might say, "Please share with me your expectations of the product's performance."
Researcher.	An overexaminer, this customer has a tendency to spin your words. Be sure to have the customer repeat the information you told them to avoid misunderstanding.

Figure 10 illustrates how personality types correlate with the need for information and how they impact a customer's decision making. For example, the talkative personality finds it

FIGURE 10 Personality types and buyer behavior

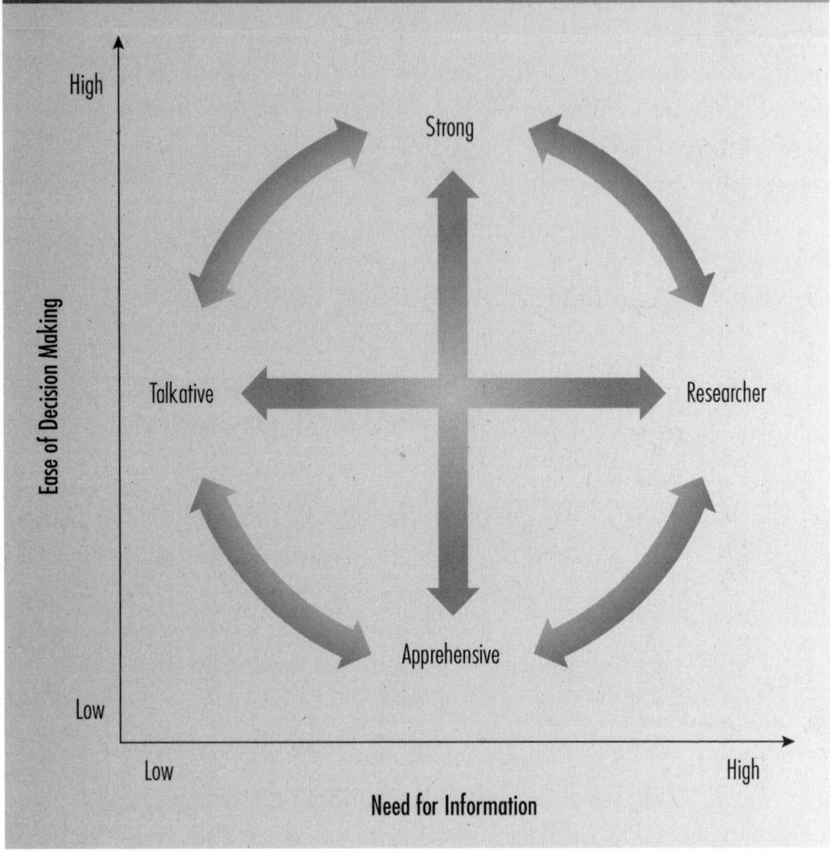

somewhat difficult to make decisions but doesn't need as much information in order to come to a decision as some other personality types do.

The Strong Personality

Strong personalities clearly and directly communicate their needs, so be prepared to respond to them with confidence and self-assurance. Be efficient, focusing on the tasks without losing sight of the goal. People with strong personalities are comfortable with risk, welcome change, and solicit input, but tend to be suspicious. Be prepared to offer innovative concepts and then back these up with facts.

The following traits indicate a strong personality type:

- direct, bold, and authoritative
- decisive decision maker
- requires facts without fluff
- enjoys the "gamesmanship"

Their buying motives include social standing, self-image, financial status, and lifestyle. You can connect with a strong personality by being well organized and concise, knowing your subject matter well, presenting with facts rather than feelings, and focusing on the end result.

Following is an example of how a sales presentation might proceed with a strong customer.

> STRONG CUSTOMER: My *Robb Report* magazine recently critiqued an outdoor kitchen setup that I am interested in duplicating for my home. I am confident that this option is available to purchase; correct?
>
> DESIGNER: Yes, we have two outdoor kitchen designs for you to select from. I will review them when we make exterior selections.
>
> STRONG CUSTOMER: I want to duplicate the design I saw in the magazine. I am sure we can accommodate that; right?
>
> DESIGNER: The home you have selected is designed with a specific backyard hardscape and our architects have designed the kitchens to work harmoniously with the space. We are not able to change the location of equipment; however, we have a wonderful selection of materials that create a very specific look. Tell me what you liked about the outdoor kitchen design.

STRONG CUSTOMER: The Viking grill, the granite countertop, and the stone wall behind the grill. How much is your summer kitchen option?

DESIGNER: It varies in price depending on the design material; however, the outdoor kitchen starts at $___. Are you comfortable with the price?

STRONG CUSTOMER: That will be fine, but I do not want to spend an excessive amount of time selecting material. I will show you what I am interested in and you just let me know the price.

The Talkative Personality

The talkative personality gravitates toward fun, trendiness, and peer recognition, so be entertaining and approachable with this customer. Do not burden them with details. Instead, applaud their creative side. Friendliness goes a long way with this personality; however, gentle control of time and process is paramount to keeping them focused. The talkative customer tells you what they want, so listen carefully and validate their choices with examples of what is current and in style.

The following characteristics indicate a talkative personality type:

- not detail oriented
- makes decisions with passion and emotion
- very animated, easily excited, and distracted
- willing to take risks, fun loving

The talkative personality is motivated to buy for amusement, reputation, aesthetic appeal, and social appeal. You can connect with a talkative personality by inspiring them with fresh ideas. It also helps to be social, matching your enthusiasm and excitement to theirs. Use pictures and visuals to validate their decisions. Keep them focused on the task at hand.

Your sales conversation with a talkative customer might unfold as follows:

> TALKATIVE CUSTOMER: My friend recently hired someone to install a summer kitchen in her backyard. Can you show me your summer kitchens? I may be interested in one for my home.
>
> DESIGNER: We have two outdoor kitchen designs for you to select from. I will review them when we make exterior selections.
>
> TALKATIVE CUSTOMER: Oh great! Let's take a look right now, and while we are at it, I would love a firepit; they are great for entertaining.
>
> DESIGNER: Unfortunately, firepits are not an available option. Are you OK with just the summer kitchen?
>
> TALKATIVE CUSTOMER: I guess that will be fine. Can I coordinate my pool tile to match the outdoor countertop? Oh, and what about a waterfall for the pool? I saw one on TV and thought that would be nice for our pool.
>
> DESIGNER: I noted the information you have told me and when we get to the outdoor area, we can review it for the proper selections.
>
> TALKATIVE CUSTOMER: Great, I can't wait. By the way, do you offer motorized window treatments?

The Apprehensive Personality

The apprehensive personality is hesitant, unrushed, and deliberate. Therefore, be supportive, informative, and provide guidance during your presentation. Treat them as a friend or family member and reassure them that their decisions are correct. Apprehensive personalities seek input and direction, so be prepared to present the solution in a manner that appears to be a collaborative effort.

The apprehensive personality type is evident in a person who

- elicits others' opinions
- is unsure of their own needs and decisions
- is sensitive, cooperative, and dependable
- avoids conflicts

Apprehensive personalities purchase for security, family, well-being, and self-esteem.

To connect with an apprehensive personality, you will need to reassure them frequently. It is also helpful to present information slowly and methodically, and demonstrate genuine interest in their concerns. Finally, be friendly and do not pressure this customer.

Following is an example of a conversation with an apprehensive customer.

> APPREHENSIVE CUSTOMER: What do you think about an outdoor summer kitchen for the backyard? I hear they are popular; are they worth the money?
>
> DESIGNER: We have a couple of outdoor kitchen designs for the property you purchased. Many of my customers have purchased the option. Do you think you will use your outdoor area for entertaining and cooking?
>
> APPREHENSIVE CUSTOMER: I guess so. How often do people use the kitchen? Is cleanup a problem? What about bugs?
>
> DESIGNER: As with any area that involves food and entertaining, there is some maintenance involved. Do you prefer low-maintenance living?
>
> APPREHENSIVE CUSTOMER: I prefer a simple environment, without constant maintenance.

DESIGNER: I think you may be interested in viewing our mobile grills for outdoor cooking and entertaining. They attach directly to the gas pipe and are ready to go. Let's review them when we are making the exterior selections, OK?

APPREHENSIVE CUSTOMER: That's a great idea! It sounds better than the whole-kitchen idea.

The Researcher

Researchers, as the name implies, are logical, precise, and want to know the details, so be well prepared, well informed about the product, and methodical in your presentation. Above all, be accurate, as this personality type does not tolerate mistakes or wrong information. The researcher asks many questions and wants to know why things are the way they are, so be tolerant of their inquiries and conservative with your suggestions. Give them what they want.

The following indicate a researcher personality type:

- asks many questions
- well versed on the product
- serious, judgmental, and not overly social
- perfectionist, realist
- detail oriented

The researcher personality wants a home that is functional, affordable, comfortable. This customer is interested in value-added options.

You can connect with the researcher by presenting them with the facts, speaking clearly and concisely, using research to support logic, and presenting the information incrementally.

Your dialog with a researcher customer might go as follows:

RESEARCHER CUSTOMER: I spent some time investigating the details of an outdoor kitchen and decided it is an option I would like further information on.

DESIGNER: We have a couple of outdoor kitchens designed specifically for your floor plan. We can review these in detail when we select the exterior options for your home. Did you happen to bring the information you found with you?

RESEARCHER CUSTOMER: Yes I did. In addition, I prioritized the items I want. I have specific questions about the grill and its workings and warranty.

DESIGNER: That's fine; we have manufacturer specifications on the grill that I can give to you. These provide detailed information on the grill, such as dimensions, material, installation information, and more. I think you will find it a comprehensive package.

RESEARCHER CUSTOMER: My primary concerns are its cost and functionality.

DESIGNER: We have a floor sample in the showroom. It provides a very good idea of how to operate the grill. Regarding price, we have two sizes available to suit different budgets. I will review them with you.

RESEARCHER CUSTOMER: That will be very helpful.

Take time to learn how to recognize and connect with the personality profiles and understand why they buy. Identifying your customer's personality type and then connecting with their buying style will help you engage them. Studies show that customers who are engaged are more likely to purchase products, because they know that their interests are your primary concern. It's all in the relationship; make the connection and build the sale.

Success will breed success as you hone your sales techniques according to the basic personality types. You will satisfy more customers with the home options they want. They will be happy to pay to customize their home to meet their individual needs and their satisfaction will lead to referrals.

Being a Better Listener

Short of handing them a personality test to fill out, one way to understand a home buyer's personality is to listen to and watch them. Therefore, before you try to sell anything, learn to ask customers the right questions and then actively listen to their responses and be aware of their body language.

Relationship selling is the most effective type of sale, and the only way to build a relationship is to hear what the other person is saying. In sales, listening skills indicate that you are engaged and interested in your customer's needs. These skills build the foundation for a successful relationship with a home buyer. When a customer knows that a salesperson is listening and working in their best interest, they relax and become comfortable offering more information that will help you fulfill their needs. Comfort, trust, and confidence build a strong customer-salesperson relationship.

Active Listening

When your customer answers a question, paraphrase their answer to show that you heard them, then ask them clarifying questions. But be careful: allow your customer to finish speaking before you begin to respond. Note the following three examples:

Example 1: Learn to Repeat

CUSTOMER: I want to create an outdoor area that my family can enjoy and that will be practical and easy to maintain.

SALESPERSON: I understand you are interested in an outdoor area that is family friendly and functional. Will a summer kitchen be part of the plan?

CUSTOMER: Oh, we would love an outdoor cooking area. That's a great idea, we never thought about that!

Lesson 1: By repeating the request, the salesperson shows the customer that they understand the need. With further clarification, the salesperson can increase the sale and ultimately exceed the customer's expectations.

Example 2: Let Them Finish

CUSTOMER: The kitchen countertop is very important to me . . .

SALESPERSON: Oh, wait until you see the new granite colors that just arrived. They will be perfect with your color scheme. Let's take a look!

CUSTOMER: Oh, no; I don't like granite. We had it in our last house and did not like the maintenance aspect.

Lesson 2: Not letting the customer finish her thought led the salesperson in the wrong direction. Rude behavior such as interrupting can be a relationship killer and spell trouble for your option sales program.

Example 3: Apply Your Knowledge

CUSTOMER: The kitchen countertop is very important to me. We regularly cook and entertain in the kitchen, so the countertop needs to be durable, yet good looking.

SALESPERSON: We have a couple of different products that will meet your needs. Do you like a stone look?

CUSTOMER: I don't like granite. We had it in our last house and did not like the maintenance aspect.

SALESPERSON: Let me show you another product that resembles granite but is much easier to maintain.

CUSTOMER: Oh, great! Let's take a look.

Lesson 3: By letting the customer finish her sentence, the salesperson was able to get further clarification on the true need. With this information, the salesperson was able to suggest the appropriate option and sell the upgrade.

Helping Customers Hear You

Sometimes customers themselves have weak listening skills. Learn to identify customers with poor listening skills and use the following techniques to ensure that you are heard and understood.

Example 1: Provide Direction

While you are discussing a cabinet and countertop design for the kitchen, the customer interjects: "I really like the window treatments on the window over there. What colors are available?" This is an indication that the customer is distracted and you risk losing control of the sale. Your winning technique is to bring the customer back to the present with the following techniques:

- Acknowledge their comment.
- Reassure them that you will address their specific need later in the appointment.
- Emphasize the importance of completing the current task and explain how it will make the next selection easier.
- Review the initial plan to regain their attention.

Example 2: Remain Calm

While you are reviewing notes about kitchen design from a previous conversation with the customer, the customer comments, "You didn't tell me that the lighting was not part of the kitchen package. I assumed it was included in the price."

This indication of selective listening may happen again, so don't engage in "I said/you said" conversations. Instead, respond to this and any future occurrences of selective listening as follows:

- Gently clarify the facts.
- Empathize with the customer. For example, use phrases such as "I understand how you feel," "Others have felt," "We have found."
- Explain what is feasible.
- Confirm the customer's agreement.
- Be firm and confident, avoiding phrases such as "I think," "sort of," or "I guess," which make you appear to be uncertain and uninformed.

Example 3: Keep Moving

As you are recapping and/or confirming various selections, the customer remarks, "That's good, so how much longer will this take?" The customer is becoming bored and frustrated. You are losing their attention. Bring the customer back with the following techniques:

- Pick up the pace of your presentation and the selections process.

Improving Your Listening Skills

Do you really care about the customer and the sale, or are you just in sales for the money? Your customer will be able to tell. You communicate caring in what you say, how you say it, and how you look when you say it. The following five guidelines will help you communicate caring by being a good listener:

1. Close your mouth and open your ears. Do not plan what you are going to say next while someone else is talking.
2. Take notes. If the customer is taking time to tell you things, take the time to remember them.
3. Repeat answers. Show your customer that you clearly understand them by acknowledging their responses.
4. Make eye contact. Look at the customer when they are talking to you.
5. Do not predict the results. Stay in the moment and let the process evolve, rather than assuming an outcome.

- Explain what remains to be accomplished and how it will benefit them.
- Use their name frequently.
- Stick to your previously established ending for the appointment.
- Ask if they would like to take a short break.
- Make your points succinctly. Don't ramble.

Nonverbal Communication

Listening to their words is only one way of discovering what a customer is thinking and feeling. Learn to read their body language, and manage your own, as part of the art of selling. Table 2 summarizes how to read and react to a home buyer's body language.

Certain nonverbal habits will help engage the customer. Practice them as follows:

- Smile and speak in a responsive tone.
- Shake hands firmly, but not aggressively.
- Stand or sit up straight.
- Use fluid motions; avoid fidgeting and tapping.
- Maintain eye contact with the customer and others present at the appointment.
- Nod your head to validate what the customer is saying.
- Be neat and polished, with professional attire and limited accessories.
- Keep your glasses clean if you wear them.
- Be relaxed, open, and demonstrate your commitment to and interest in the customer by showing emotion.
- Take off your jacket and roll up your sleeves to communicate your desire for an open and reciprocal relationship.

Can You Hear Me?

93% of communication is nonverbal:

- 55% is body language
- 38% is tone of voice

TABLE 2 Reading and reacting to a customer's body language

Customer Posture and Interpretation	Your Winning Technique
Standing with hands on hips may indicate a challenge or impatience and anxiety.	*Gain agreement!* Interrupt your presentation to ask your customer if they are satisfied with what is being presented.
Tilted or cocked head may indicate interest and agreement.	*Go for the close!* Confirm that the needs have been satisfied.
Arms crossed on chest may be a defensive position and may also indicate the customer is uncomfortable.	*Gain clarification!* Ask clarifying questions such as, "What are your thoughts regarding this selection?" Use information the customer provides to redirect the presentation.
Wide-open eyes and head jerked back may indicate surprise and doubt.	*Take notice!* Acknowledge the reaction by opening up discussion about what caused the surprise.
Hand to cheek or chin may indicate the customer is evaluating what was just presented or discussed.	*Let there be silence!* Try not to fill in every silence with words. Give your customer time to absorb the information and ask the next question.
Rubbing hands together may signify the customer has different expectations and may seek an alternate plan.	*Be flexible!* Invite your customer to share their ideas. Listen to their input, without interrupting, and if feasible,

TABLE 2 Reading and reacting to a customer's body language (*continued*)

Customer Posture and Interpretation	Your Winning Technique
	incorporate their suggestions into the overall plan.
Sitting with hands behind head may indicate confidence and dominance.	*Stay focused!* Don't let the posture fluster you. This position may appear intimidating but does not necessarily mean that any change in presentation style is necessary. Continue with the message.
Removing eyeglasses and fiddling with the arm of the glasses.	*Slow the pace!* Recognize that your customer is interested and thinking about what was just presented. Slow down and elicit questions.

Selling to Couples

Selling to more than one decision maker is different from selling to an individual. In most cases, you are presenting to and attempting to close the sale with more than one personality profile. Because of their profiles and other issues, they may disagree or struggle to come to a decision. Follow these five steps when communicating with and closing a sale with more than one personality type.

1. Encourage couples to review the option selections prior to meeting with design staff so they can discuss and prioritize choices privately.

2. Speak to both parties throughout the presentation.
3. Remain calm and be ready with possible solutions to disagreements.
4. Don't take sides. Instead, acknowledge both decision makers and work to find common ground.
5. If necessary, encourage couples to meet privately when they reach an impasse.

Feature and Benefit Selling

Uncovering a customer's personal perception of value is the key to unlocking a sale. Words such as "pretty," "fancy," "high-tech," "wonderful," or any other adjective you might apply to home features will not sell your products. Customers purchase items they value. In other words, features tell, but benefits sell! What do they deem worthy, useful, important? Quality, warranty, functionality? To meet a customer's needs, your job is to find out what they value. Only then can you explain how a product's features align with a particular value and how these will benefit the customer. Features are the characteristics that describe the product. Benefits are the value-added attributes of a product in the customer's eyes.

When talking to customers about product features, focus on

- product detail, including colors, materials, and other attributes
- mechanical detail, such as automation
- warranty and service details

When discussing benefits of a product, focus on how it

- meets a need
- solves a problem
- proves to be the best in the market
- is the better price value

Let's examine how a skilled salesperson turns features into benefits that align with a customer's values and helps them decide to buy.

Example 1: The Wrong Way to Sell

> CUSTOMER: We are very interested in natural-looking materials for the floor, but just as important, we need durability and ease of maintenance because of the children and pets.
>
> SALESPERSON: Let me show you the new porcelain product that just arrived. It is a little bit more expensive; however, it is really great looking and it comes in many colors. I think you will like it!
>
> CUSTOMER: Well, what do you mean more expensive? We had previously decided that we were not going to spend a lot on the flooring.
>
> SALESPERSON: OK, how about if we use the porcelain in just the kitchen and laundry room. We will use the included flooring in the remaining areas of the house and this will not affect your budget.
>
> CUSTOMER: Oh no, that's OK. I think we will just stay with the included flooring throughout the house and upgrade it after closing.

Lesson 1: Confusing money with value immobilizes customers. By raising cost first, rather than the long-term value of porcelain to the customer, the customer naturally focused on budget as well, rather than durability and maintenance. The salesperson did not explain that porcelain would meet the customer's needs and add value to their lifestyle.

Now, let's see how to sell the same product correctly to the same customer.

Example 2: The Right Way to Sell

CUSTOMER: We are very interested in natural-looking materials for the floor, but we also need durability and ease of maintenance because of the children and pets.

SALESPERSON: Let me show you the new porcelain product that just arrived. This flooring looks like natural stone, is incredibly durable, and is easy to maintain. It is perfect for your lifestyle. It will provide you the natural look that you really like and low maintenance—perfect for the children and pets.

CUSTOMER: Great! That's a good suggestion because minimal maintenance is very important to us. Let's take a look. How much more will it cost?

SALESPERSON: It may be a bit more expensive; however, you will be very pleased with the performance of the material in the long run.

CUSTOMER: A few dollars more is not a big issue if we like it. Let's take a look!

Lesson 2: The salesperson maintained customer focus on the value of the product, while still answering the home buyer's question about price. Thus, money remained secondary to product value in the buyer's mind.

The Power of Suggestive Selling

Customers often do not know which options are available or which ones they really need. Suggestive selling is the art of inspiring customers by expanding a single product purchase into a "total concept" sale. This strategy allows you to offer an array of products that respond to your customer's lifestyle needs.

To become a pro at suggestive selling, take a customer's vision from fantasy to reality by

- asking the right questions
- patiently listening to customers' answers
- suggesting the right product for the customer
- diligently and creatively offering various product choices

New home buyers are often pressed for time and overwhelmed with the number of decisions they have to make before they can move into their homes. Be patient and guide them through the process. In addition, with budget high on consumers' minds, only sell your customer the options that they value and that they can afford. Helping your clients design homes that comport with their lifestyles and budgets will help build trusting relationships and bring in greater option dollars.

Follow these seven guidelines to master the art of suggestive selling:

1. **Know your product and its features.** Learn all of the key product features so that you can present them as benefits to the customer. Customers will view you as a knowledgeable resource.
2. **Learn what your customer wants.** This enables you to make relevant product suggestions. Link product features to customers' needs so that the customer understands the value of what they are purchasing.
3. **Rehearse product presentations and keep them simple.** If your presentation is stilted and stiff, rather than natural and effortless, customers won't believe what you are saying. As the array of products and home technology options expands, remember to avoid industry jargon. Instead, communicate product features and benefits in plain language that the customer will understand.

4. **Time product suggestions to the customer's pace.** A sound product suggestion, offered at the wrong time, can kill a potential sale. Be on the lookout for clues that your customer is overwhelmed, confused, or unable to make a decision. Rather than pressing on after you notice these barriers, skip to another area of options and revisit the product offering later. Above all, maintain a relaxed atmosphere even as you work to generate excitement for products.
5. **Be assertive, not aggressive.** Suggest options with confidence and poise, explaining why you believe the products best suit the customer. Listen to customer concerns and don't discount their beliefs and values. Strong, dominating behavior breeds separation and resistance and can kill sales.
6. **Remember your perceptions are not your customer's.** Therefore, don't let your ideas about money and value get in the way of selling high-end or luxury options. Just because you don't see value or can't afford a product does not mean the product would not suit your customer's taste and budget.
7. **Overcome the fear of rejection.** View each "no" as a stepping-stone to acceptance and another opportunity to get to know your customer better.

Example: Suggestive Selling Done Right

During your preappointment contact with the customer, you discover they are very interested in health and fitness. Prior to the appointment, you should develop a list of health-related options to suggest. Following is an example of how the presentation might proceed:

> SALESPERSON: I would like to ask you a few questions about your drinking water preference before we finalize the kitchen design. You mentioned that

drinking water is an important aspect of your family's health. Do you currently buy bottled water?

CUSTOMER: Yes, we do.

SALESPERSON: There are several good brands of bottled water and many of my other customers have purchased bottled water. However, I would like to suggest our new in-house filtration system. It provides great tasting, chemical-free water that won't make your skin dry. It can be run throughout the house, not just the kitchen, and may help you save money. Is this something that interests you?

CUSTOMER: You know, that is a good idea; it may save trips to the store. Tell me more.

Lesson: Note that the salesperson successfully used information about the customer that was gathered previously to apply during the design presentation. Only then did the salesperson discuss the product's features and benefits. The salesperson presented these clearly and then asked for customer agreement.

Suggestive selling allows you to increase sales by satisfying customers' needs. In working with home buyers to select options, you are selling lifestyle and vision, not just discrete products.

Learn, Practice, and Apply

In sales, and in any situation where you are trying to communicate with another person, your speaking style and how others perceive what you say are as important as the words you use. Moreover, customers don't care what you know unless they know that you care, so listen to them and demonstrate that you are hearing what they are saying. Learn, practice, and apply the techniques in this chapter and watch option sales grow.

6

Handling Objections and Closing

Selling begins when the customer says "No!" Therefore, to be successful in option sales, you can't let rejection rattle you. Customer objections are a natural part of the selling process. In addition, remember that closing culminates a natural progression that begins when you first meet the customer, take time to get to know them, and then present options that are the best fit for their lifestyle and budget. A successful presentation encompasses

- identifying and connecting with personality types
- perfecting listening and body language skills
- communicating value
- selling vision
- managing expectations
- providing above average customer service

Starting with "No"

Although our egos may naturally gravitate toward positive responses, the negatives help us better understand the home buyer. In most cases, an objection is just a signal that your customer is apprehensive about committing to a decision. You can overcome apprehension by understanding the reason behind the "no" response. Table 3 lists possible reasons for a customer objection, how to interpret it, and techniques for overcoming it.

TABLE 3 Handling objections

Customer	Objection Interpretation	Your Winning Technique
Does not understand a product's features and how it benefits them.	Customer needs further information and education on the product.	*Be patient and acknowledge their comments.* Offer additional information that will explain how the product satisfies their needs.
May openly reject the price or disguise the price objection with another reason.	Customer believes the price is not in line with the value of the product.	*Stay positive and nondefensive.* Connect the value of the product with the customer's needs. Clearly communicate the benefit. In certain situations, you may ask "Why do you think it is too expensive?"
May say "we really do not need that" or "that is not important to us."	Customer believes that their needs are not being addressed.	*Uncover the customer's needs by asking questions such as:* "Why do you feel . . . ?"

(continued)

TABLE 3 Handling objections (*continued*)

Customer	Objection Interpretation	Your Winning Technique
		"What is it about . . . ?" Then redirect your presentation.
May show agreement to the product but hesitate to make the commitment	Customer is close to a decision, but a concern still needs to be addressed.	*Recap all of the decisions made throughout the presentation and regain agreement.* Ask for clarification about why they are hesitating.
May show indecisive behavior and seek input from others	Customer may be fearful of making an incorrect decision.	*Empathize and reassure them; then, share other customer's experiences and the positive results.* Example: "I understand how you feel. Others have felt the same way but found that . . ."
May show signs of shutting down with a "fear-frozen" gaze	Customer may be overwhelmed with the process.	*Seek to understand the customer's needs.* Recap and connect them back to the original enthusiasm for the product. Then, move to confirm which products meet those needs.

Common Customer Objections

Following are two examples of how to handle common customer objections regarding price and included product that arise in option selling.

Example 1: Option Price

CUSTOMER: That is too expensive. Let's just stay with the standard and I will deal with it after I close on the house. I am sure I can get a much better price.

SALESPERSON: I understand your concerns, but let me explain why the price is more than you expected. Many considerations determine the total price of this option package, including warranties, sales tax, installation, and delivery charges. All optional features are rolled into the mortgage and ready for you to enjoy after closing; you won't have to deal with the inconvenience and disruption of remodeling after you have moved in. Wouldn't it be better to enjoy your home from the day you move in? When you consider what it would cost to add these items individually and the added convenience of having your home complete prior to moving in, you will find that this is a very competitive price.

CUSTOMER: Great! Let's do it!

Example 2: Included Product

CUSTOMER: So tell me, what I am getting for the money I spent on the house? I don't understand why I have to pay more for my cabinets or flooring or other items. Why are these items not included in the price of the house?

SALESPERSON: The homes in the community (or neighborhood) are predesigned with a specific group of products. Since these items are purchased in quan-

> tities, we are able to offer you the house at this favorable price. We also give you the option of personalizing your home by offering other choices at an additional cost. These packages provide you the opportunity to create a home that reflects your and your family's lifestyle.

Objections are not rejections. Instead, they are a signal to uncover the cause of hesitation and pursue the relationship. Review and become skilled at the preceding techniques so that you are prepared when your customer presents objections.

How to Close a Design Presentation

To minimize surprises, maximize value for the customer, and build a successful option selling program, practice the art of mini-closing. Through mini-closings, you gain agreement from the customer throughout the sales process.

The Opening Close

The opening close occurs at the beginning of the design center appointment. In chapter 4 we discussed the importance of reviewing and confirming information gathered from the customer prior to their design appointment. Use this as your first opportunity to close. After reviewing the information from your customer, simply ask if they agree. For example, say, "We have reviewed everything that was discussed and have agreed on all items. Are you comfortable with that?" If your customer says "yes" you will move on to select options. However, they may have a different response. A possible alternate scenario and a suggested response follows:

> DESIGNER: I have reviewed everything discussed and decided upon from our telephone call. Do you agree? Do you have any further questions? If you are in agreement we will move forward.

CUSTOMER: Actually, we have changed our mind about the third bedroom and decided to create a home office.

DESIGNER: OK; let me write that down and we will look at the available home office options later in the appointment.

The Category Close

Because option sales are built on concept selling and selling a concept requires selling multiple products, the best technique is to secure agreement at multiple points in your presentation. Studies indicate that the more a customer says "yes," the clearer the path is to the final close. Consider the following example:

SALESPERSON: Before we move on to the next area of your home, let me confirm that you are comfortable with the selections we have just made.

If your customer is comfortable with the selections then you will move on to the next area of product selections. However, the following might occur instead:

CUSTOMER: I am concerned that the backsplash we selected is too expensive and in order to stay within our budget, we will have to forfeit other options that are important. I think I will eliminate the backsplash completely.

SALESPERSON: I understand; let me show you an idea for the kitchen backsplash that reduces the cost without compromising the mood of the kitchen design.

CUSTOMER: Oh, that's great. If it works and I like it, we can use the money we save for the home office. Thank you for understanding our budget concerns, we really want a nice home office, with custom cabinetry and all.

This technique is most effective when applied for each option category throughout the presentation.

> **Guidelines for Getting to Yes**
>
> **Empathize with the customer** by using phrases such as "I hear you saying . . ." or "I appreciate that . . ." Then, help your customer reach a decision.
>
> **Demonstrate your active listening skills** by restating the customer's objection and asking for clarification. Ask questions such as "Why do you think . . ." or "What do you mean by . . . ?"
>
> **Focus on how an item relates to an overall concept or lifestyle,** creating a vision your customer can grasp.
>
> **Work with the customer to gain agreement** on solutions in a series of "mini-closes."

The Final Close

Securing customer buy-in at various milestones makes for a trouble-free and straightforward final close. Because everything has been agreed upon along the way, both parties know what to expect and there are no surprises.

The final close begins with a review of option selections and ends with the customer signing necessary paperwork and paying the required deposit. For example, the salesperson would say to the customer: "Now that we have completed the selections and agree on the final design, let's move forward with the paperwork. We will review it together and then all I need is a signature and a deposit and we are ready to go."

Closing Clues

The following behaviors indicate that a customer is ready to close:

- **Feature/benefit summation.** The customer recaps the details of a particular product and then seeks your validation.

- **Performance questions.** The customer asks specific questions about how a particular product will perform or how it meets their needs.
- **Requests for repeat.** The customer asks for further information or clarification about a particular product that has been discussed.
- **Open body language.** The customer displays nonverbal clues such as smiles and friendliness, pulling their chair closer to the table or moving closer to you, and nodding their head when you speak.
- **Product participation.** A customer shows interest in the product by reviewing product information, or touching and interacting with the product.

Avoiding Surprises

Closings do not have to be surprise endings if you are methodical in your presentation and ask for customer agreement in mini-closings along the way. By fully disclosing all of the information about your products and services, your customer has the facts to make educated decisions. You become the educator helping your customer make decisions with comfort and confidence. Furthermore, identifying and understanding your customer's buying signals will help you ask for the sale at the perfect time.

7

Providing Customer Service

Providing stellar customer service can set your company apart and increase customer loyalty and referrals. Unfortunately, good customer service appears to be a luxury that many people do not experience today. Consider the following:

During a design center appointment, Ted, the customer, asked Sara, the design salesperson, about products, procedure, cost, and other items. As she proceeded to answer his questions, it became apparent that Ted had received inconsistent information from other sources. The home sales team had informed Ted that his new home came with standard stone flooring throughout the main areas. Sara had community information in front of her stating that porcelain, not stone, was the standard flooring. This was a recent change, initiated by the community manager but apparently not communicated to the home sales team. Ted told Sara that he was unhappy about the confusion; however, he was still interested in having stone floors and asked how much more it would cost. Not only was Sara unable to provide a price for the upgrade to stone, she could not commit to a time when she would have a price. Ted was frustrated, as you can imagine.

Even though she could not resolve the flooring issue, Sara eased Ted forward with the selection process. Ted had more questions—about the selection process, available options, prices, and when the option contract would be completed. Because she had received only a partial option list and only a few prices, Sara could not answer any of these questions. She did not know when to expect the options and price lists, but she told Ted not to worry, and assured him that everything else would run smoothly. She acknowledged his frustration and encouraged pressing on with selections. He pulled out his wish list. At the top of the list was a steam shower, a favorite feature in his previous house! Sadly, Sara had to tell Ted that a steam shower was not an option, even though she knew it was a popular feature for consumers.

Like most customers, Ted wanted to feel happy about his home purchase and confident that he had chosen the right builder. However, this last denial of his lifestyle preference pushed him to the brink.

Sadly, Ted's story is not an isolated incident in the home building and design industries. In fact, many customers have endured arduous processes for creating their dream home and have expressed similar frustrations.

What can we learn from this example of poor customer service? Good customer service encompasses much more than a smile and a handshake. The entire company—not just the sales and design departments—must work together to create a clear path to customer satisfaction. As all builders know, purchasing a home involves passing through multiple phases, beginning in the sales office and ending at the closing table. The customer moves from department to department and person to person. Your success in moving customers from one stage of the home buying process to the next affects customer satisfaction and impacts your referral rate. To maximize the customer experience and ensure that customers are prepared to fully experience the design process, ensure that their transition from one phase to another is pleasant and uncomplicated.

It is vital that the transition between each department be seamless. Use the design center department report, other reports described in chapter 3, and regular meetings to facilitate communication among departments. Invest in a Customer Relationship Management (CRM) program for creating a seamless flow of customer information. Sound home building company practices, back-office processes, and field supervision provide the foundation for all employees, uniformly, to alleviate customer concerns, reduce frustration, inspire customer confidence and excitement, and generate revenue.

The Path to Customer Satisfaction

Following is an example of a 10-step path to ensure that the option process is smooth and critical information is exchanged and shared appropriately.

1. The customer purchases a home at the sales center.
2. The community sales representative contacts the design center to schedule a design appointment while the customer is present. (This eliminates playing "phone tag" with a customer.)
3. The sales center provides the design center with copies of key pages from the customer's contract and any addenda specifying details such as elevation changes or option credits.
4. After receiving the contract, the design center sends the customer an orientation packet to introduce the design center and its process.
5. The design center receptionist or design assistant creates the customer file and assigns a designer via a rotation system.

6. The designer contacts the customer for a preappointment telephone introduction.
7. Using information gathered during that telephone call, the designer prepares for the design appointment.
8. The designer meets with the customer, reviews the design process, recaps information gathered in the telephone conversation, and secures selections.
9. Before ending the design appointment, the designer sets customer expectations for the next step and reviews company policy on making changes to the option contract.
10. The designer secures a deposit and customer signature on the option contract, copies it, and gives the copy to the customer. The original hard copy is filed in the customer folder; it is also scanned into or posted on the company's shared network, along with drawings or specific instructions.

Customer Relationship Management

CRM is not just a technology, but a company-specific, customer-focused strategy for servicing the customer through each phase of the home purchase. Ensuring unity and common purpose among internal systems improves a company's ability to serve its customers well.

Every employee or contractor working with your company contributes to the customer experience. If you currently do not have a CRM program, use the welcome letter, orientation packet, option selection process tools, frequently asked customer questions, and customer service quiz in this book to begin to create one. Keep all departments informed with an Active Customer Report (tool 15) as shown in figure 11 to set the stage for better customer service and fewer mistakes. Coupled with the design center department report discussed in chapter 3, it is the first step toward sound customer management.

FIGURE 11 Active customer report (tool 15)

Active Customer Report								
Week of: 3.17.08								
Today's Date:	Customer Name	Neighborhood	Lot/Unit # Floor Plan	Contract Date	Designer	Appt Date	Comments	Start Date
3/17	McNulty	Nob Hill	2/Estate	2/9	Sara	15-Feb	Option contract finalized and signed by the customer. Operations manager to process the contract on 3.19	
Community Name								
Today's Date:	Customer Name	Neighborhood	Lot/Unit # Floor Plan	Contract Date	Designer	Appt Date	Comments	Start Date
3/17	Squire	Chelsea	24/Bella	3/12	Sara	1-Apr	Design center appt scheduled	
Community Name								
Today's Date:	Customer Name	Neighborhood	Lot/Unit # Floor Plan	Contract Date	Designer	Appt Date	Comments	Start Date
3/17	Anderson	Larkspur Lakes	17/Terra	3/14	Sara		Left message to call studio to schedule appt.	

The active customer report provides real-time information to all departments involved in and affected by option selection. The template included on the companion Web page to this book was created as an Excel spreadsheet but the report also can be created in your automated CRM system. Maintain the report on a shared network so that all designers can enter comments on the progress of the option selection process and community, sales, construction, purchasing, and closing managers can view it. If a shared network is not feasible, you can e-mail the report to the necessary staff.

Under the design center manager's direction, the receptionist enters the following information into the report when a home sales contract is received at the design center: customer name, subdivision, lot/unit number/floor plan, contract date, designer name, and design center appointment date.

The report should be updated every Friday afternoon and reviewed by design center management on Monday morning. The "Today's Date" and "Week of" entries should correspond. The "Contract Date" column indicates the date of the home purchase contract (not the options contract). The home contract date reveals whether customers are being processed through the design center in a timely manner. Tracking this date helps ensure that home buyers are not left unnoticed or unattended. Teach your designer to use this tool to manage the customer base and the option selection process. Be sure to date and update it each week.

During busy periods, the active customer report may grow to 10 or more pages, although all of the information does not necessarily change from one week to the next. The purpose of requiring designers to change the "Today's Date" entries as the report is updated is to assure the reviewing manager that the information is current. Likewise, prior to sending the report to other departments, the manager updates the "Week of" date to assure other managers that the report is current.

Customer Folder

Because the time period between a customer's first design center contact and closing can be more than a year, accurate and detailed written records are a must. A customer folder and file system with forms, design appointment option checklist, active customer report, and the design center department report discussed in chapter 3 are organizational tools that work with automated systems.

Keep customer contracts, diagrams, e-mail, other correspondence, and other documentation neatly organized in a color-coded folder for professional presentation and easy access to information. Designers, managers, and warranty representatives will use this folder to confirm or clarify pricing and other details. Use a heavy-stock, top-tabbed folder with pronged self-adhesive fasteners to create a usable four-sided folder (fig. 5).

Use one color per community. The folder may be legal- or letter-sized, depending upon the documents. Organize the folder as follows:

Inside Front Cover

1. Customer Contact and Community Information Cover Sheet (tool 16). Print this form on your company letterhead. Insert it on the inside front cover of the customer folder, so that the designer will know at a glance whose customer he or she is working with.

FIGURE 12 Customer folder layout

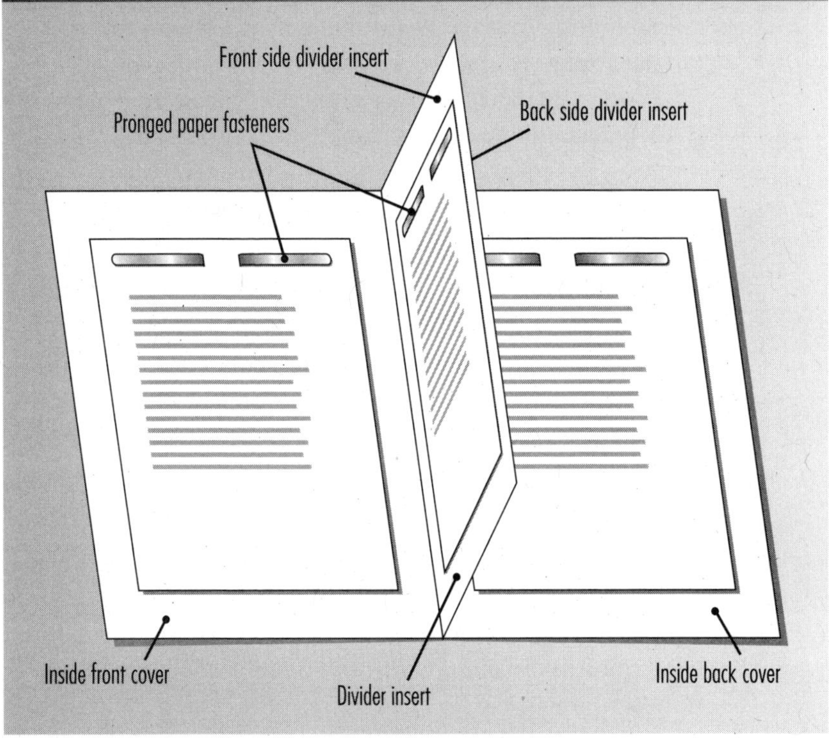

2. Completed customer contracts should be placed behind the Customer Contact and Community Information Sheet and accompanied by:
   - floor plan (with each room's floor covering identified)
   - electrical plan
   - diagrams and/or photos
   - copy of check deposit
   - correspondence, e-mail messages, letters from the customer

Divider Insert—Front Side

1. Record of Customer Correspondence (tool 17). Print this form on your company letterhead. The design center receptionist will insert it in the folder. It will be used to

record all design center and customer telephone and meeting correspondence. This documentation will include both the dates and details of conversations. Because purchasing a home involves multiple steps, the form will help track over time the many conversations with customers that impact their design choices. If you want to be remembered for your excellent customer service, then you must make the effort to get to know and remember your customer!

2. Contract Information Cover Sheet (tool 18) and materials disclaimers, signed by the customer. Place these items behind the record of customer correspondence. The contract information cover sheet alerts the design center of a home sale and need to schedule a design center appointment. Blank forms should be kept at the sales center. Salespeople should be instructed to complete one after each home purchase. Have sales center staff e-mail or fax the completed form and its attachments to the design center. This process ensures that the design center receives the customer information, proof of purchase, and other pertinent information about the home purchase.

The materials disclaimer details specific characteristics of products used in the home and recommended care. It also includes company policies and warranties. It is included in the orientation packet. The designer should secure the customer's signature on the disclaimer before placing it in the folder.

Divider Insert—Reverse Side

Place price lists, quotes for custom work that falls outside of your typical options offerings, and option product information here.

Inside Back Cover

Keep records of e-mail correspondence and photos of palettes as a reference should questions arise regarding products, colors, and designs the customer requested or selected.

Managing Customer Expectations

Managing customer expectations takes the courage to attentively serve, rather than merely to please. There is a direct relationship between what a customer expects to happen and what they perceive has happened after the experience. In other words, the expectations they have bear directly on whether they leave satisfied. If their perceived experience is better than what they expected, they are a happy, satisfied customer. Conversely, if their perceived experience is less than what they expected, they are an unhappy, unsatisfied customer. Therefore, your goal is to manage a customer's expectations so that you consistently exceed what they expect. Do this by clearly communicating, from the beginning of the relationship, what your customer can expect from their home buying experience. Use the procedures discussed in chapter 4 to manage customer expectations and to anticipate customers' questions so you can better serve them.

Admittedly, today's customer has high expectations regarding services and products. However, you can satisfy their desires while managing these expectations. The following guidelines can help you reap rewards in profits and referrals.

Review Processes

Take time to review your processes at the beginning of the customer relationship. This will set the stage for realistic expectations and allow you to correct any misinformation. The orientation packet is the first step in setting customer expectations. The preappointment telephone call is another early opportunity.

List and Discuss

Make a list of common misconceptions and routine challenges for new customers, and then discuss these openly with the customer. For example, one common frustration is the level of detail required in selecting options. Preparing the customer for this saves time and promotes their confidence. Clearly communicate to the customer the importance of reviewing the orientation packet, and suggest that the customer note any questions they have as they review the book. Encourage your customer to preview your product offerings before their design center appointment. Stress the importance of bringing photos of favorite rooms that reflect their lifestyle and living habits.

Communicate Clearly, Consistently, and in Writing

Customers often become confused about available options because they receive conflicting information. Take time to clearly define your option program and what changes are permitted; have this information in writing, and make sure staff uses it. If the company manual states that no changes are permitted after the options contract is signed, then don't undermine the company's reputation by telling the customer that you can issue a change order after that. Avoid industry jargon in your discussions with home buyers and in your written materials for them. For example, say, "inventory home," rather than "spec," write "new construction" rather than "TBB," and discuss "available features" rather than "upgrades."

Organize Everything

If you find it challenging to keep up with design options, imagine how your customer feels! He or she is probably a novice in the home design and construction process. Make it easier for customers by preparing, and helping them prepare, for their design appointments. Again, the orientation packet is a tool to help them.

Make it a Dialog

Learn your customer's expectations. After you have discussed what they can expect from your company, its processes, and promises, ask them to tell you what they expect. This open dialog affords another opportunity to head off potential misunderstandings. Confirm that your customer understands what they can expect. Gain confirmation along the way. After presenting them with information, ask them if they understand and are comfortable with what you have presented. For example, during the preappointment call, clearly outline the option selection schedule as follows: "I would like to review the schedule for completing your home selections. Your design appointment is next week and we will select all of the materials to complete the design of your home. At the end of the appointment I will finalize the paperwork with your signature and you will leave a deposit check for 25% of the total amount. Do you have any questions?"

These steps will help your company avoid promising more than you can deliver. Managing your customers' expectations from start to finish allows you to exceed them and gain satisfied buyers and referrals. Remember that what a customer shares with others can be your best, or your worst, advertisement.

Frequently Asked Questions (FAQs)

Knowing how to respond to the most frequently asked questions enhances your credibility with customers, increases your own confidence, and averts sticky misunderstandings or miscommunication. You should be prepared to respond to FAQs such as those that follow. You can add to them or develop a list specific to your company.

Q. May we make a change to the floor plan?

A. Our homes are designed for each room to work as part of a harmonious whole. The existing floor plan was created to accommodate livability, adhere to building codes, and ensure appropriate spatial relationships. (Some builders allow structural changes under certain conditions. If this is your procedure, ensure that all changes to the floor plan are documented before the design center appointment.)

Q. May we move outlets, lights, or light switches?

A. Lights, outlets, and switches are placed in accordance with electrical codes and to ensure livability. Although we cannot eliminate electrical components, we offer optional lighting packages that include additional lights and upgraded fixtures.

Q. May I get a credit on the included flooring and install my own flooring after I close on the home?

A. To protect your investment, we sell only finished homes. We allow only approved construction professionals to install flooring and other components of your new home. Therefore, we are able to include a warranty on both standard and optional components that you select. To protect this warranty, only company personnel or our designated contractors are permitted to work on our homes.

Q. I have seen my faucet for less than what you are charging for the same faucet. Why is there a price difference?

A. Our price includes taxes, labor, delivery, and a warranty on all material and labor. Every effort has been made to price our products competitively; however, we do not always have the same buying power as other retailers.

Q. What is the closing date for my home?

A. At this time, we are unable to provide you with an exact closing date. However, we understand the importance of planning your move and we estimate construction of your new home will take [state estimated number of weeks]. As construction of your home progresses, we will provide you with an estimated closing date within [state estimated number of days] of your closing.

Q. Will I be able to make changes during the building process?

A. No, that will not be possible. Once you select the optional features you want and our design center processes the paperwork, no changes or additions will be permitted.

Get Personal

Of course, the reports, file folders, and checklists will be meaningless if the frontline staff alienates customers by being inattentive. Pamper your customer with first-class customer service. "The customer still wants that old mom-and-pop store treatment woven in with today's technological marvels. They listen to the warmth or absence of it in a phone call," says Shannon Larsen, editor of *Option* magazine.[18]

Customer Service Do's and Don'ts

Do

- Be patient with uneasy or unsure customers.
- Smile and reassure customers.
- Show customers how important they are, including responding to important messages immediately.
- Explain all procedures, processes, and realistic expectations at the beginning of the relationship.
- Use customer friendly language and avoid trade lingo.
- Be gracious and respect your customers.
- Contact the customer within the promised time frame, even if you do not have the answer.

Don't

- Overreact or take personal affront with an angry customer.
- Send a frustrated customer elsewhere; you will only further frustrate them!
- Blame an angry customer or act in a condescending manner when they become emotional.
- Avoid being responsible for solving a customer's problem.
- Keep reciting the rules to make your point when attempting to correct misinformation given to a customer.

Table 4 lists responses that create a negative impact on your customers and some alternative phrases that will have a positive impact.

Measure Your Customer Service Prowess

To test your company's customer service prowess, take the quiz that follows. (Answers and more explanations for handling these scenarios begin on page 113.)

1. You respond to a customer asking "What is my next step?" as follows:
   a. I don't know . . . I suggest you call this person; they should know.
   b. Let's review the handbook . . . it provides all the information you need.
   c. What would you like to do next?
2. Your customer leaves an important telephone and/or e-mail message, you respond
   a. within 48 hours
   b. the same day
   c. whenever you happen to get around to it
3. Your customer is questioning one of your procedures. You respond
   a. "It is what it is."
   b. "I don't understand it either; that's not my area of expertise."
   c. "I think it will help you if I explain how the procedure works . . ."
4. Your customer is being indecisive. You
   a. smile and reassure them
   b. walk away frustrated
   c. tell them that time is running out, so it is important to make a decision

TABLE 4 Words that make a positive impression

Negative Impact Phrases	Positive Impact Phrases
I don't know.	I do not have the answer right now. I will take some notes and will get back to you [state a time frame] with the correct information.
Oh no, that cannot be done.	Unfortunately, that is not possible; however, we may consider this alternative.
Sorry; it is what it is.	I understand how you feel; however, we are unable to accommodate the request at this time. I understand what you are saying and want you to know I am here to help.
No, you did not tell me that.	Thank you for bringing that to my attention. I don't recall discussing it. Let us take some time right now to review the information.
I don't have a choice in the matter.	There are a couple of ways to approach this. What do you think of . . . ?
You will have to.	May I suggest . . . Here is what I am able to do . . .
This is the only way it should be done.	In my professional opinion, our best options are . . .

5. A customer calls you after leaving unanswered messages for other staff members. You
   a. tell the customer their issue is another department's responsibility and they have to work through that department
   b. tell them you will look into it and call them back with information as soon as possible
   c. tell them you will call them back with information, but never do so

6. Your customer has a special request that the company cannot meet. Your response to them is
   a. "Oh, no, we can't do that!"
   b. offering a comparable and feasible alternative
   c. a chuckle, followed by, "I wish!"

7. Your customer arrives 25 minutes early for an appointment. You
   a. acknowledge them graciously and tell them you will be available shortly
   b. let them wait; it's not your fault they're early
   c. approach them and tell them you are busy and there is no way you can meet with them before the scheduled time

8. You have finalized the details of the sale and collected the money. When your customer later calls with questions, you
   a. help when you have time but don't make it a top priority
   b. ignore the call with relief because now you can focus on your other customers
   c. welcome the call and let the customer know that you are available to assist throughout the entire process

9. Your customer calls you about something that you clearly forgot to do. You
   a. explain that you inquired about this, but no one ever got back to you

b. apologize, accept responsibility, and get the information immediately
c. tell your customer that you do not recall the conversation

10. Your customer is very angry about a particular situation. You
    a. steer clear of your customer until you feel prepared to approach them
    b. argue until you win
    c. empathize and talk to your customer about what can be done to resolve the situation

Answers to Customer Service Quiz

1. (b) You remain in control, guide your customer through the established process to clarify and manage their expectations, and eliminate misconceptions and misinformation.
2. (b) Important messages can change a multitude of situations. Responding the same day may be critical to your company's own processes. In addition, by responding promptly you are sending a clear message that your customer is a high priority.
3. (c) Make it a point to know and understand your company's policies and procedures. If you understand the rationale behind the rules, you can impart them clearly to the customer.
4. (a) Remain calm, reassure the customer, and review all the great choices they have made so far. Tie their choices back to their lifestyle.
5. (b) Leaving a customer in the dark, without answers, causes frustration and makes the customer feel unimportant. Seek out the answers and promptly call the customer back.
6. (b) As the Rolling Stones sang, "You can't always get what you want, but if you try . . . you get what you need." Try to identify the customer's need and then present an alternative solution.

7. (a) Immediately greet your customer and graciously explain that you will be with them shortly. Offer them something to drink and a comfortable place to wait.
8. (c) It is important to the company's reputation that a customer feels like they are a top priority. Therefore, you must be available throughout the building process. Never give the impression that now that you made the sale, you don't have time for your customer.
9. (b) Be honest. Your customer will appreciate that you admitted your error. Follow up promptly and work hard not to repeat the mistake.
10. (c) Remember to let the customer know that you are always working in their best interest. Avoid company bashing. Instead, creatively and proactively resolve the issue.

Have Customers Grade You

Your customers can provide valuable information about how they perceived their design center and option selection experience. Send the design center Customer Survey (tool 19) within 30 days of the customer finalizing their option contract at the design center. Or, have the receptionist or designer present the survey at the conclusion of the options process, along with a self-addressed, stamped envelope. Ask the customer to return the survey within one week. If you choose to have them mailed, schedule one day each month to do so. Use the design center department report to track the dates surveys were mailed and reviewed.

A Competitive Edge

Although they have many choices of builders in today's highly competitive environment, customers are starved for good service. Therefore, companies that consistently provide outstanding customer service and high-quality products will outshine their competitors and continue to grow revenue. On the other hand, lack of attention to detail, compromising quality, and giving below average customer service will put companies at a disadvantage, damage their reputations, and send potential customers elsewhere. Now, more than ever, is the time to provide a high level of customer service that differentiates you from your competitors. BuilderBooks offers several books on providing excellent customer service, including *Beyond Warranty: Building Your Referral Business* and *Building Your Home: An Insider's Guide, Second edition,* both by Carol Smith, a well-known customer service expert.

Conclusion

Making the most of every home sale means learning to sell effectively to consumers' individual lifestyles. Today, you must think like a retailer in order to give customers what they want. That means doing your best to excite them about purchasing options that are tailored to their particular vision of themselves and their new homes.

Create a design and option selling program that will appeal to your target market—whether that means starting your own center, using a model home, or working through a third party. Examine your current sales tools, business-planning tools, and customer service tools. Purge outdated practices that are no longer workable and replace them with fresh, new, and innovative ones that meet today's home selling demands.

By following the guidelines presented in this book and using the tools provided on the Web page you will be well on your way to creating a program that will be an asset to your home building business for years to come.

Notes

1. John Mc Manus, "Design by the Numbers," *Big Builder,* July 2005, 6.
2. Jason Knott, "Making Options Magic" *TecHome Builder,* October/November 2007, 34.
3. Chris McDonald, co-owner and vice president, The Artisans Group, in interview with the editor, April 2008.
4. Kristen Nillsen, co-president, Gold Medallion Homes, in personal communication with the editor, April 2008.
5. "Home Technology Disconnect Could Mean Lost Revenues," *Nation's Building News Online,* April 21, 2008.
6. Keith Davis, "Like Builders, ESCs Specialize in Different Market Segments," *Nation's Building News Online,* April 21, 2008.
7. Gretchen Palmer, co-owner, Palmer Homes, in personal communication with the editor, April 2008.
8. Cheryl Weber, "Arriving at Customer Central," *Big Builder,* July 2005, 17.
9. Susan Werner, "5 Ways To Boost Design Center Efficiency," *TecHome Builder,* March 2007, 34.
10. See note 3 above.

11. Peter G. Merrill, president and CEO, Construction Dispute Resolution Services, LLC, in personal communication with the editor, February 2008.
12. Terance Manly, design studio manager, Winmark Homes, in discussion with the author February 2008.
13. Cheryl Weber, "Urban Options, *Big Builder,* July 2005, 35.
14. See note 5 above.
15. Cheryl Weber, 36.
16. See note 12 above.
17. Ross Robbins, "Sales Makers vs. Order Takers" *NAHB, The Members Directory,* 2007, 29.
18. Shannon Larsen, *Option Magazine,* July/August 2007, 14.

Resources

1. *BDC Magazine Quarterly*
   www.bdcmagazine.com
   Magazine for people who design, develop, and operate builder and independent design centers

2. *Options For Today's Fine Homes*
   www.optionsmag.com
   Magazine for home builders that includes product listings and information about design centers, service providers, and industry associations

3. *TecHome BUILDER*
   www.techomebuilder.com
   Magazine focused on business and home technology products and services

4. 20/20 Technology
   www.2020technologies.com
   Design software company that provides computer-aided design and sales for the design industry, including three-dimensional visualization of kitchens and baths

5. Virtual Solutions
   www.3dvs.com
   Architectural marketing firm that works with state-of-the-art technology to help increase sales and upgrade options
6. Pivotal CRM
   www.pivotal.com
   Industry-tailored customer relationship management system, designed around the entire customer lifecycle
7. Envision
   www.builderhomesite.com
   Fully integrated options management solution
8. Think Construction Suites
   www.constructionsuite.com
   CRM for small-to-medium-sized businesses
9. SC Design New Home Interiors
   www.scdesigninc.com
   Full-service licensed design center for the building industry
10. CTI
    www.ctihome.com
    Interiors partner to the builder industry

Index

D

F

G

H

I

J

K

L

M

N

O

P

R

S

T

V

W

About the National Association of Home Builders

The National Association of Home Builders is a Washington-based trade association representing more than 235,000 members involved in home building, remodeling, multifamily construction, property management, trade contracting, design, housing finance, building product manufacturing, and other aspects of residential and light commercial construction. Known as "the voice of the housing industry," NAHB is affiliated with more than 800 state and local home builders associations around the country. NAHB's builder members construct about 80 percent of all new residential units, supporting one of the largest engines of economic growth in the country: housing.

Join the National Association of Home Builders by joining your local home builders association. Visit www.nahb.org/join or call 800-368-5242, x0, for information on state and local associations near you. Great member benefits include:

- Access to the **National Housing Resource Center** and its collection of electronic databases, books, journals, videos, and CDs. Call 800-368-5254, x8296 or e-mail nhrc@nahb.org
- **Nation's Building News**, the weekly e-newsletter containing industry news. Visit www.nahb.org/nbn
- **Extended access to www.nahb.org** when members log in. Visit www.nahb.org/login
- **Business Management Tools** for members only that are designed to help you improve strategic planning, time management, information technology, customer service, and other ways to increase profits through effective business management. Visit www.nahb.org/biztools
- **Council membership**:
  - **Building Systems Council**: www.nahb.org/buildingsystems
  - **Commercial Builders Council**: www.nahb.org/commercial
  - **Building Systems Council's Concrete Home Building Council**: www.nahb.org/concrete
  - **Multifamily Council**: www.nahb.org/multifamily
  - **National Sales & Marketing Council**: www.nahb.org/nsmc
  - **NAHB Remodelers**: www.nahb.org/remodelers
  - **Women's Council**: www.nahb.org/womens
  - **50+ Housing Council**: www.nahb.org/50plus

BuilderBooks, the book publishing arm of NAHB, publishes inspirational and educational products for the housing industry and offers a variety of books, software, brochures, and more in English and Spanish. Visit www.BuilderBooks.com or call 800-223-2665. NAHB members save at least 10% on every book.

BuilderBooks Digital Delivery offers more than 30 publications, forms, contracts, and checklists that are instantly delivered in electronic format to your desktop. Visit www.BuilderBooks.com and click on Digital Delivery.

The **Member Advantage Program** offers NAHB members discounts on products and services such as computers, automobiles, payroll services, and much more. Keep more of your hard-earned revenue by cashing in on the savings today. Visit www.nahb.org/ma for a comprehensive overview of all available programs.